LIKEWISE. *Go and do.*

A man comes across an ancient enemy, beaten and left for dead. He lifts the wounded man onto the back of a donkey and takes him to an inn to tend to the man's recovery. Jesus tells this story and instructs those who are listening to "go and do likewise."

Likewise books explore a compassionate, active faith lived out in real time. When we're skeptical about the status quo, Likewise books challenge us to create culture responsibly. When we're confused about who we are and what we're supposed to be doing, Likewise books help us listen for God's voice. When we're discouraged by the troubled world we've inherited, Likewise books encourage us to hold onto hope.

In this life we will face challenges that demand our response. Likewise books face those challenges with us so we can act on faith.

ivpress.com/likewisebooks
twitter.com/likewise_books
facebook.com/likewisebooks
youtube.com/user/likewisebooks

Christine Jeske
and Adam Jeske

This
Ordinary
Adventure

SETTLING DOWN WITHOUT SETTLING

IVP Books

An imprint of InterVarsity Press
Downers Grove, Illinois

InterVarsity Press
P.O. Box 1400, Downers Grove, IL 60515-1426
World Wide Web: www.ivpress.com
E-mail: email@ivpress.com

InterVarsity Press® is the book-publishing division of InterVarsity Christian Fellowship/USA®, a movement of students and faculty active on campus at hundreds of universities, colleges and schools of nursing in the United States of America, and a member movement of the International Fellowship of Evangelical Students. For information about local and regional activities, write Public Relations Dept., InterVarsity Christian Fellowship/USA, 6400 Schroeder Rd., P.O. Box 7895, Madison, WI 53707-7895, or visit the IVCF website at <www.intervarsity.org>.

All Scripture quotations, unless otherwise indicated, are taken from THE HOLY BIBLE, NEW INTERNATIONAL VERSION®, NIV® Copyright © 1973, 1978, 1984, 2011 by Biblica, Inc.™ Used by permission. All rights reserved worldwide.

While all stories in this book are true, some names and identifying information in this book have been changed to protect the privacy of the individuals involved.

Cover design: Cindy Kiple
Interior design: Beth Hagenberg
Images: Title type, church photo, girl on bike and dirt bike/rainbow: Christine and Adam Jeske
    sofa: © Tyson Wirtzfeld/iStockphoto
    Art Nouveau frame: © ben phillips/iStockphoto
    copper and steel frame: © ben phillips/iStockphoto
    painted frame: © ben phillips/iStockphoto

ISBN 978-0-8308-3787-8

Printed in the United States of America ∞

Library of Congress Cataloging-in-Publication Data has been requested.

P	21	20	19	18	17	16	15	14	13	12	11	10	9	8	7	6	5	4	3	2	1
Y	30	29	28	27	26	25	24	23	22	21	20	19	18	17	16	15	14	13	12		

Contents

1

DENTED DISHWASHERS

BECOMING ORDINARY

Adam

Chrissy was whacking a butcher knife on the top rack of the dishwasher. I sat stunned on the couch across the room, unable to quite make out whether she was using the blunt edge of the knife or the sharp. In our eleven years of marriage, I had never seen anything like this from Chrissy. I figured we could deal with the dings in the dishwasher rack later, as long as Chrissy didn't throw the knife at me.

"We're not amazing anymore!" she shouted, loudly enough that I hoped the kids had fallen asleep quickly. "I'm sick of trying to have all these great adventures. I'm sick of trying to do something amazing every day, because I can't. I can't do it. My life is boring." Whack!

I let out a breath. *This is it,* I thought. *It's all unraveling. She's right.* We'd been back in Wisconsin for ten months, after years traipsing around the globe as do-gooders. The normalcy was strangling us.

The day of the knife incident was my birthday. I had turned thirty-three—a third of a century. Until that moment, I believed the day was going pretty well. Some coworkers had surprised me with ice cream sandwiches just before the end of the workday. When I got home, Chrissy was arriving from schlepping the kids across town to pick up a last-minute gift, a sweatshirt that turned out to have sleeves too short for my chimpy arms.

But the other presents she and the kids found were all winners—a stainless-steel travel mug on clearance, a secondhand book that Phoebe picked out and argyle socks from Zeke. In addition to last-minute shopping, Chrissy had also taught piano lessons for three kids that afternoon. She ran out of time for a birthday cake, but I genuinely didn't mind.

We ate fish for dinner, deliciously flavored with parsley and lemon. The meal provided some semblance of elegance and cele-bration in that quick hour between greeting each other and leaving again as a family for the kids' first elementary school open house in the United States. At the open house, we admired our children's crooked letters and drawings of kites and enjoyed seeing their names printed on their very own cubby holes, amidst the flocks of other moms and dads in yoga pants and suits. Now back at home, a simple "How was your day?" had somehow prompted not the happy birthday musings I hoped for but rather this whirlwind of electric angst.

"I'm sorry, okay? I'm sorry!" Chrissy seethed. "I want to be amazing, but I can't do it. I hate it."

She paused, and I knew she had more to say. After eleven years of marriage, I'd learned enough to know when not to interrupt (at least sometimes). And I knew where she was coming from, because I sud-denly realized that I was in the same place. I wanted to reassure Chrissy, "We're doing great. Our life here is remarkable—we're helping more people than ever, we're living some great stories, we're not like everybody else!" All lies.

For years, we had been trying to live a life charged with energy and risk, trying to do good as we lived in four very different coun-tries around the globe, avoiding the shackles of the status quo. We attempted to make every day amazing or even just notice how it already was amazing. We had traveled around the world, and the last thing we ever wanted to do was keep up with the Joneses. Instead we had become the Joneses. My international adventure muscles had atrophied. My intensity had waned. I needed to stop denying it: I had been domesticated.

■   ■   ■

On the autumn day when we met fourteen years earlier, when I was a freshman in college, I had plopped down at a university cafeteria table beside a friend, right next to Chrissy. In our first conversation there I explained that I was so happy that I had just rolled down a hill, giggling all the way, with the kind of extreme joy normally reserved for preschoolers. "That makes today an Amazing Day," I told her. Since some time in high school, I had been using the term *Amazing Day* to describe anything that made a day unusual, silly, daring, faithful, wacky or bold. Little did I know, we would remember that day for something far more amazing than my roll down the hill.

As young newlyweds, we show off T-shirts a friend gave us as a wedding gift.

Apparently, my two mismatched, argyle, over-the-calf socks, orange shorts and general zest got Chrissy's attention. What I didn't realize about this demure and freckled beauty was that she was more than up for any adventure I could concoct. She wanted to live adventures that mattered. And we would live those together.

Two-and-a-half years later, a week after Chrissy's graduation and a year before mine, we got married. We scrawled the words *Amazing Days* on a sheet of paper and taped it to the side of our refrigerator. We refused to be that couple who dried up into crusty old people (or worse yet crusty young people) who would drive their fifty-minute commutes to jobs jabbing at keyboards and checking off phone calls and never looking anybody in the face or leaving any glint of meaningful improvement on this world. We had both given our lives to Jesus years before, and we believed that gave us an excuse to do more than just trudge through life waiting to land in heaven someday. We trusted that God had saved us to glorify him here in the present, and that meant embracing whatever adventures God led us into as we offered to serve him each day.

So our Amazing Days list grew over the weeks and months to include such strange events as these. We

- invited runaway street kids over to make soup
- gathered friends together for a meal consisting entirely of fried foods
- read the entire New Testament aloud in one sitting
- befriended Sudanese refugees
- gave out carloads of day-old bread
- explored a labyrinth of tunnels under the University of Wisconsin
- fasted
- made soap out of lye and the fat of a deer I killed
- sold hundreds of dozens of Krispy Kreme donuts to support Habitat for Humanity
- made snow angels

The Amazing Days list was like a beacon in the center of our home reminding us to always stay romantic, silly, adventuresome, attuned to divine promptings and beyond-a-shadow-of-a-doubt alive. Intentionally living and tracking Amazing Days drew us out of the mundane ruts of life and into small (and large) attempts to make the most of life.

In August 2000, fourteen months after our wedding and three months after I finished my degree, we moved to a Nicaraguan village. We were full of wide-eyed faith, ready to learn what it was like to live in abject poverty, to discover how to make an impact in the world and to find out what on earth Jesus meant when he said the words, "Blessed are the poor."

After a year back in the United States, we left home again to spend all of 2003 and 2004 in China, where we taught English to future English teachers.

Next, after spending the 2005-2006 school year working at the University of Wisconsin in Oshkosh, we took a shared position as microfinance project managers in rural South Africa using the M.B.A.s we'd gotten along the way. Later, in 2008, we moved to a seminary in Pietermaritzburg, South Africa, and taught intercultural communication, leadership and economic development.

By the time we moved to South Africa, we had two small children, Phoebe and Zeke. At ages three and five, Zeke and Pheobe were already shouting "Amazing Day!" when they found shells on the beach, spotted a hawk, made the "world's tallest" Lego tower or went swimming in thier underpants in a river rumored to have crocodiles in it.

And the Amazing Days list grew. Many Amazing Days came easily when we lived overseas. New experiences sprang upon us like surprises behind the doors of a carnival fun house, complete with a few scary clowns. Someone cas-trated a pig in Nica-

Settling into "ordinary" life, Adam savors reading time with Zeke after work.

ragua, and I found myself holding a surprisingly large still-pulsating pig testicle in each hand. Friends invited us over for a pot of deer soup with the deer skull and antlers floating in the center of the pot. Chrissy and the kids knelt by the side of a South African road to change our sixth flat tire in a month. Chrissy stopped at a friend's house to drop off some hand-me-down children's clothes and learned that the friend had just taken an HIV test that came out positive. I cried while preaching through a Zulu interpreter to five hundred people in a concrete-block church. I rode a motorcycle across the mountainous African country of Lesotho in a day, taking over twenty hours and crashing twice, including once with a sheep.

I liked rocking around the world, for sure. But for Chrissy, our time in South Africa was the fulfillment of nine years of longing to get to the continent. At the UW, she'd taken courses like African Storyteller and Global Malnutrition (even as an English Literature and Piano Performance double major), and she knew she eventually needed to get to somewhere in Africa. While I was happy to be there and sensed a calling, Chrissy loved it with a passion—she had found her dream job. After years of waiting, she was living it. It was everything she'd hoped for.

And then we had to move back to the boring old United States of America.

■   ■   ■

Throughout the years, our refusal to be normal led to great stories. People invited us to speak at colleges, churches and Rotary lunches. We were profiled in the second largest newspaper in Wisconsin. A newspaper in Oshkosh asked Chrissy to write a column about life in South Africa. We won an award from the University of Wisconsin for outstanding alumni under the age of forty. We wrote about our adventures and insights for magazines.

Our life led to stories. Our stories led to audiences. Our audiences led to more adventures. It was a positive feedback loop. We grew accustomed to living differently and telling about it, in writing and in person.

I went back to an old hobby—photography—to tell stories more visually. And Chrissy wrote a book about the people we met in South Africa and issues of international development.[1] The book got published, and we set up a speaking trip around the United States to tell stories of the beautiful people we'd met around the world. Life was great.

The end of our work commitments in South Africa coincided with the release of that book. Phoebe and Zeke were six and four, easy ages to start over in a culture in which neither remembered living. Chrissy was ready to start applying for Ph.D. programs in anthropology, and the time was ripe to reconnect to family members we'd seen only once a year for too many years. We moved back to our home state of Wisconsin, a place where few internationally recognized decisions of global importance are made. It is not Washington, D.C., New York or even Seattle. Wisconsin was famous only for cheese and perhaps *Little House in the Big Woods*, Jeffrey Dahmer and the Packers, if those count as famous.

We quickly realized that here there were no adrenaline-pumping rides on tottering overfilled buses to remind us we were glad to be alive. After we had been back in the U.S. for a while, our friends no longer gushed with the overused words "so radical" when describing our lives. We settled down as thirty-somethings with kids but hadn't entirely figured out how to play the role. We didn't want to be the nutjobs known for making our own ponchos, keeping seventeen birdhouses or heating our home by burning cherry pits (not that there's anything *wrong* with ponchos, birdhouses or cherry pits).

We wanted to live a life that was good, satisfying and amazing, not boring and not *too* weird (at least not weird in the wrong ways). It seemed like there was no time, no space, no energy to live the kind of life I wanted. The Amazing Days list had gotten mashed into a box of papers somewhere in the process of moving and still had never made it back onto our refrigerator.

■   ■   ■

Chrissy balanced a clean frying pan upside down to dry on top of a pile of plates and bowls, next to the butcher knife. "I'm tired of trying to write what everyone else wants, to *live* what everyone else wants. I can't make everyone happy."

Chrissy was spending the first year back in the United States applying for graduate schools while freelance writing, blogging and speaking. A few days before my birthday, a writing agent had replied to her email by asking her for more "oomph to impress publishers," more of what he called "wow stories." He asked what things we had done that others would dare not try, what experiences would give us a platform to write about living an amazing life, even back in the U.S. It wasn't bad advice, just bad timing. I knew the "wow stories" pressure had something to do with this birthday meltdown.

"So write what you want to write," I offered, staring at the coffee table and biting my lip. Maybe I could diffuse the situation, make room for other options, deflate this angst balloon. I feared where we were headed—either giving up on writing or giving up on something bigger.

"I don't *know* what I want to write! Maybe the problem is I'm not just trying to write what everybody else wants; I'm trying to *live* what everybody else wants too. And that doesn't work either. I would love to do something meaningful and write about it. Writing is supposed to unfold as we live, but right now there's nothing unfolding. Life is stuck. We're stuck."

She set a bowl under the faucet and waited for it to fill. When we moved into the apartment the water pressure in the kitchen seemed strangely low, and then a week ago, the pressure suddenly dropped to a trickle. To fill a glass of water, we would either walk to the bathroom sink where the pressure was better or set the glass under the kitchen tap, leave for a few minutes and come back to fetch the water. To get hot water, we would wait the length of time it took to rinse all the dishes. The water was probably just starting to come out hot now. Patience was taut.

"I hate trying to write while doing nothing." She swished a brush around the last bowl and tucked it over some plates in the dishwasher.

"Well, fine—so scrap it." I took off my glasses and pressed my fingers into my eyes until I saw red and purple blasts. I squeezed the skin of my temples together. I hoped this conversation would be one tiny, tiny prick in the angst balloon, allowing some pressure to escape without causing a blowout. "Set it aside. Do whatever you need to do. Go get a job—it's fine."

"I . . . have *not* . . . the *least* idea . . . what kind of *job* . . . I would *get*." She spit out the words in bursts, punctuated by a slam of the dishwasher and the crank of the dial to "Normal Wash."

Maybe the problem wouldn't be that easy to solve, even just for tonight.

■　　■　　■

As Chrissy was whacking the dishwasher, it had been ten months since our return from South Africa, and that angst balloon had been filling ever since. We spent the first six months on what we called a "sabbatical," a mix of rest, fun, job-hunting, and wondering what in the world God was doing with us, where we would end up and what we would do to feed and house our family. Coming back to the U.S., we didn't have jobs, a home or a heap of other things a family of four is expected to have—a car, a second car, career paths, a school district, a kitchen table, beds, bicycles, iPhones, a printer, Barbies, kiddie soccer teams or an address. So we moved into a doublewide trailer that a church provided to people in ministry in transition and spent six months alternately traveling to speak and looking for our future work and home.

A typical day looked like this: Phoebe walked ten minutes to the bus stop, rode the bus thirty minutes to school and came home eight hours later, exhausted but elated from another big day of first grade. Zeke bopped between printing letters in workbooks, sculpting Play-

Doh and swatting at Wiffle balls in our living room, cherishing every moment of attention we could give him.

Between those moments with him, Chrissy and I sat in front of computers at desks on opposite ends of the trailer, silently seeking our places to belong in the vast faceless world, then sneaking onto Facebook for the closest thing our computers offered to real faces. Chrissy researched Ph.D. programs to apply for in the coming year, which meant preparing to take the GRE entrance exam, finding recommendations and convincing strangers that she was capable of a significant intellectual contribution to the universe.

I sent job applications into the web-o-sphere, ducking over to Chrissy's end of the trailer now and then to ask if it was worth applying to jobs in Arkansas, Oregon, Texas and other places far from family where we knew no one. I tried to pray but mostly ended up pacing. Chrissy blogged and waited anxiously for someone to comment. I drummed up photography gigs for myself, using skills I'd gained while in South Africa. We squeezed in time to write query letters and articles for magazines, a waiting game of faceless communication that felt like applying and reapplying for new jobs every single day. Amazing Days seemed a hazy and distant memory, something only for the other side of the planet, for a previous season of life.

While overseas, we had interacted daily with neighbors, familiar shopkeepers, and people who knew our children's names, ages and favorite knock-knock jokes. We had limited (or no) access to the Internet, computers, cell phones, reams of activities or even electricity at times, but our life felt sustainable. There were awful, desperate times, but generally, our work captured our hearts and that grace carried us through. Life felt reasonably balanced, significant and tied to others' lives.

Freshly back in the United States, on many days we spoke to no one but our own family, and rarely did we hear anything in response to the applications and queries we poured out. I wondered if our

Amazing Days had only sprouted because they were in rich, cross-cultural soil. Maybe the context was amazing, but we were not.

Every week brought a new onslaught of questions, explicit or not: "Who are you, and what right do you have to say your skill is worth anything here? You see, we are a people of excellent standards and you are not the type to measure up here. This isn't some small pond. We are a big pond here, and you had better be something *very* special."

Eventually, I made it through the onslaught of options and self-doubt, or so it seemed. I found a job working as an associate director of communication for InterVarsity Christian Fellowship, a large nonprofit that serves college students and faculty. I started my new eight-to-five job just as school got out for the summer, and we moved into a newly rented small apartment back in Madison, Wisconsin, where we had met during college. Chrissy's days became a blur of zoo visits and library times with Phoebe and Zeke, amidst keeping up on emails, playing phone tag to set up play dates, buying closet organizers, greasing bike chains, and keeping the rice and raisins swept off the kitchen floor.

I usually got home at 5:15 if traffic was smooth, 5:30 if it wasn't, or later if meetings ran late, which meetings often do. This was the first time I'd had this kind of eight-to-five routine, and I was starving in it. My belly was ballooning as I traded my African running regimen for ever-increasing hours in my cubicle, and the cold weather was coming on fast and stealing even my few hours a week on a bicycle. Weeknights became filled with soccer and baseball games, shopping for spatulas and secondhand chairs, and exhaustion on the couch. After the kids went to bed, our conversations seemed to consist of 70 percent catching up on appointments and work, and 30 percent being too tired to say much of anything.

We did what we could to invite friends over for dinner and desserts, and we discovered peers running in the same tiresome gerbil wheel—friends acknowledging they might never reach the level of income their parents had, friends unemployed, friends having their third or fourth child, friends settling into the jobs they would have until retirement but still wondering what happened to dreams of travel, love or adventure.

Everyone was so busy. We were all "connected" through screens—especially social media and increasingly while on-the-go—but rarely were we in the same room together. We had "friends," but few real friends. We couldn't remember the last time someone unexpectedly dropped by the house. People seemed to find YouTube far more entertaining than the people nearby. Everyone seemed to want comfort, and we saw more money flowing through people's hands than in most places around the world, but very few of us seemed to *be* comfortable. Very few seemed to have gained any peace. Here, we could find out what was happening anywhere in the world at any moment, but we didn't have the time, the energy or the connection to really care.

Our friends, like us, grew up hearing that the world was our oyster, but now we felt more like we were drowning in a vast ocean, wondering if maybe there wasn't any pearl after all. We were living in places that never felt like home, working hard to prove something but finding that nothing ever seemed proven and no one ever seemed to love us more or even give a rip. We were looking around and feeling ever smaller in the sea of other nameless faces in a globalized, webtastic world.

I was tired. And Chrissy was whacking the dishwasher with a butcher knife. Maybe I should join her.

■   ■   ■

Chrissy rubbed her wet hands on her jeans and slumped onto the couch next to me. "I think I just miss being good at something. I want to feel like what I do matters to some other human being on the planet."

I opened my mouth to say the obvious, but she beat me to it.

". . . besides my kids and husband and God." She sniffled.

Between the snot and the butcher knife, Chrissy wasn't sending out very lovable vibes. But I wrapped my arm around her and shut off my attempts at quick solutions. I knew sometimes I was her partner in rising up to unleash a new flurry of Amazing Days and sometimes I was her nemesis, the very picture of normalcy, keeping her bound and boring. She curled into me like a chilled wet puppy in a blanket.

2

The Last Hurrah

LEAVING ADVENTURES BEHIND
Chrissy

The motorcycle lurched and coughed, then fell eerily silent. We slowed to a stop on a dirt road somewhere between a Kenyan village and my bus ride home.

"Oh Jesus," Mike prayed simply, barely audibly. He sat staring blankly at the handlebars for a moment. Then he turned the ignition. The motorcycle purred back into action.

As our speed climbed back to well beyond what I thought prudent, he shouted back at me through his helmet. "What time is it?"

I released my left hand long enough to check my watch. "We have ten minutes!" I shouted. Ten minutes until the one bus of the day passed by the city nearest Mike's village. Ten minutes until in missing that bus I missed the university class I was supposed to teach the following day in Uganda.

It had been half a year since our family moved from South Africa back to the United States, throwing ourselves into the tension of carving out an identity and a purpose for ourselves in middle-class North America—an identity that would somehow take into account all we'd seen and learned in years around the world. Now for just two weeks I had been invited back to the continent of Africa to teach a course called Economic Development of Developing Countries for Eastern University with students from around the world gathered in Uganda. Before the class, though, I took up an offer from a dear friend from Kenya to visit his home village and speak with some local leaders about development options in their com-

munity. Though I was still thousands of miles from our old home in South Africa, I cherished this opportunity to travel in Africa again. If all went well with the class in Uganda—including arriving in time to teach it—I hoped to return to Africa in coming years to

Somewhere along the Indian Ocean on holiday, friends humored us long enough to snap this photo while we tried not to fall off the truck in gusting winds.

teach the class again. Missing that bus could mean losing my chance at returning to visit friends like Mike, pushing life back in the United States just one nudge further toward the mundane.

"I think we might make it!" Mike rolled the throttle to its max.

I clamped my legs tight against the sides of the bike and clenched my fingers on Mike's jacket. I kept my eyes on the ruts and rain gullies that crisscrossed the road like veins, only occasionally glancing up at the fields of dry corn stalks and the low umbrella leaves of cassava plants speeding past.

Mike shouted over his shoulder, "We'll be fine, as long as the engine doesn't cut out again when we're going fast!" I wasn't sure how it could happen when we weren't going fast, since fast was all we were going.

Bam! Mike and I both flinched at the gunshot sound coming from somewhere behind or beneath us. My fingers dug into his sides.

Bang! The blast went off again. This time we looked down at our own vehicle, recognizing the sound as the complaint of the motorcycle's tailpipe.

The motorcycle continued letting out its sporadic muffler explosions every thirty or sixty seconds. As we barreled down the dirt road, I prayed the kind of prayer that has often been prayed in Africa: "God protect the handlebars, and God protect the brake pads, and God protect the brake fluid line, and God protect the gearbox, and God protect the carburetor."

Mike leaving church on his motorcycle

Somehow reviewing the parts of Mike's very well-used fifteen-year-old 185cc motorcycle in prayer only left me gripping his sides more tightly. I couldn't shake from my mind the picture of what would happen if God didn't protect the handlebars, the brakes, the chain, the tires. The best scenario was we'd sit by the road for a while waiting for help and miss the bus but have some lovely story to tell of Kenyan hospitality along the roadside. The worst scenario was my bare arms, legs and helmetless head would meet Kenyan gravel—or a Kenyan grave.

How long would it be before my husband, Adam, and our two children, Phoebe and Zeke, heard the news back in the United States? I imagined a phone ringing back in Wisconsin, Zeke looking up from balancing a Hot Wheels car on a towering parking garage of blocks, Phoebe looking up from a book on origami or second-grade spies, hearing their grandma answer the dreadful phone call from Kenya. This line of thinking was not helping.

As scared as I was, though, I had to admit that in exchange for security, riding helmetless offered a great thrill. Wind cooled and enlivened my face as I soaked in the full view of mud brick homes, chickens, goats, stretches of corn, cassava and peanut fields. Even here on the decrepit motorcycle, I couldn't help smiling. If today was my day to die on a Kenyan road, at least it had been a fine way to spend the last few days. And like any good movie should, this story was climaxing in a wild, high-speed chase scene punctuated by gunfire, or at least what sounded like it.

I straightened my back to see over Mike's head, releasing the fear-knotted muscles of my spine and telling myself what a nice story this would make. I began mentally scripting the email I would write home to Adam whenever I next saw a computer. I imagined concluding my email home, "Today was a day to remember I'm still alive. And today counts as an Amazing Day."

■   ■   ■

Like many short trips to foreign countries, the trip felt like a triple-shot of espresso for the soul. In this fast-forwarded amazing race I could experience many of my favorite—and least favorite—aspects of overseas life all crammed into just four days. Arriving on the continent at 9:00 p.m. after over twenty-four hours in airplanes and airports, I had waited an hour for a friend's lost luggage, changed money, purchased minutes for my cell phone and spent every last one of those minutes trying to find someone with a key to let me into my guest house. The guest house staff had forgotten to leave me bottled water, so I took my malaria pill with a swallow of bread and brushed my teeth with a dry toothbrush at 11:00 p.m. and then discovered a coffeemaker and stayed up running a pot of tap water through it twice to purify it. The next morning I found the hot water disconnected from the bathroom, took a freezing shower and ran to catch a bus before dawn. Next came the six-hour bus ride to Mike's village, but I remembered little of it thanks to a jetlag-induced coma.

Amidst the challenges, and partly because of the challenges, the trip had also been time to tune my ears to the Holy Spirit's promptings. At the village, in conversations over locally grown tea with heaps of luxurious sugar and milk from the cow nearly nuzzling against my shoulder, I gathered notebooks of frantic scribbles and inspirations. If I was tempted to complain, I could see firsthand how much harsher life could get. I watched the wife in the family I stayed with hauling buckets of water home; I met local church members who had adopted orphans from their community; and I heard the fears of farmers about the rains that had been coming more irregularly every year. The days included some sweat, some waiting, some danger, and some remembering to slow down and not fret when meetings happened an hour late or not at all. I watched visitors coming and going at the home where I stayed and envied the casual connections between families and neighbors who had lived together for generations.

The half dozen meetings Mike had arranged with women's groups, church groups, agricultural cooperatives and micro-lending groups felt like joining a team of heroes fighting battles over life and death. We exchanged ideas about new farming practices, funding for their preschool, caring for orphans as HIV spread and took its toll, and keeping children in school. As always there were moments I would look back on and laugh. I found myself in conversations about vermiculture (*Wonderful! I will get some worms!*), surplus avocados (*Do you think we can sell avocado juice?*) and vasectomies (*They cut the man . . . where?*).

Here I was without husband, kids, Internet, errands and whatever other distractions make North Americans so harebrained-busy. Here, for now, zeal and gratitude came easily. Living long-term overseas had by no means included such a steady stream of action and impact as these four days, but it had been my spiritual training ground over most of the last ten years. Overseas I had learned lessons in attentive listening, generosity, community togetherness and doing what will matter for generations or for eternity. Taking these lessons home to cram them into the shape of my American life was not coming so easily.

■　■　■

"Look, here's the city coming," Mike shouted over his shoulder. "City" is a relative term in the developing world, and one may or may not include paved roads, electricity and sewage. Sure enough, the houses were getting closer together, the agricultural plots smaller, and ahead I could see an electric line drooping across our dirt road. In another minute we turned onto the city's one paved road.

Swerving between semi-trucks and public bicycles carrying two and three riders, we cut across the street to a small bus ticket office. The bus company sign outside offered just what I felt I had aplenty: "For the ride of your life."

I checked my watch. Two minutes after the hour. Mike stepped inside and I hung back, hoping he would get a Kenyan price on my bus ticket, not a jacked-up foreigner price.

He came out wearing a grim face, no ticket in hand. I mentally prepared for a night in a hotel and long apologies to my jilted students. In my heart I knew it wasn't just these I dreaded, though. I hated the thought of letting down the university and losing my chance to return to Africa in the foreseeable future. Even more so I dreaded the task I faced no matter when I caught a bus: the challenge of figuring out how to make life amazing in the land of the free, the nameless and the mundane, without the crutches of airplanes and adrenaline.

"The bus is a long way away. They say it will come in a couple hours."

"It's coming in a couple hours?"

His lips slowly stretched into a smile. "I guess we made it in time."

■　■　■

So Mike and I went out to lunch. Mike was one of those incredibly hardworking optimistic people we had often found living in the midst of grim poverty but defying all odds, the kind of person who deserved to have an entire book written of his life story. Aside from holding a job as a high school administrator and being one of the most organized and punctual people I knew (our motorcycle ride aside), he was a founding member of a multipurpose cooperative. Together, members of the cooperative were bringing unique locally adapted peanut processing equipment to the village, starting a women's lending group, running a preschool, offering the only Internet connection in the village and training rural farmers in anything from mushroom cultivation to opening savings accounts. All this grew out of Mike's and some other farmers' brainstorming, some local fundraising, grant applications and a lot of hard work.

We sat on plastic chairs outside a restaurant eating tortilla-like *chapattis* and tough roasted chicken with saucy cooked spinach. Between bites I rested my greasy fingers over the table and asked him, "If you could tell people how to live an amazing life, what would you tell them?"

He set down his chicken wing and looked past me into the road where bicycle taxis squeezed between the lines of semis waiting to cross the border into Uganda. "There's a quote," he said slowly, "from Martin Luther King Jr. It goes something like this: 'If someone hands you a broom, sweep like you've never swept before.'"

Just then Mike jumped out of his chair, ran into the street and disappeared around a semi parked in front of us. In a moment he reappeared. "Your bus! There it goes!"

I grabbed my backpack and pressed money into his hand for the restaurant and the gas home. "I don't need anything," he insisted, but I slid the money onto the table, gave a quick hug and ran.

I caught up with the bus a few blocks later where it stopped to unload passengers at the border to fill out visa paperwork. As the bus wound its way between sunny fields for the next five hours, then crawled the last two of those hours through the ubiquitous traffic jam in Kampala, Uganda's capital, I replayed Mike's words in my mind. Later I would look up the exact quote Mike had paraphrased: "If you are called to be a street sweeper, sweep streets like Michelangelo painted, like Beethoven composed music, or like Shakespeare wrote poetry. Sweep streets so well that all the hosts of heaven and earth will pause to say, here lived a great street sweeper who did his job well."[2]

At first as I thought about the quote, I glossed over the word *street sweeper* as some career from another era. As the bus rolled along, though, I realized I had met street sweepers in my life; I just hadn't ever paid them any attention. From our years in China, memories returned of walking outside early in the morning to see the teams of women in identical matching orange suits and wide-brimmed hats hiding their faces. Out with the first rays of sunlight, they would rake and sweep broken chopsticks, plastic bags, and bits of bread and noodles from the gutters. From more recently, I could recall the rumble of street-cleaning trucks with their huge spinning brushes swiping away leaves and trash outside our apartment in Madison. The driver sat invisible behind a high truck windshield. Aside from having to park my car on a certain side of the street once a week to stay out of their way, I had never given a street sweeper a thought. I had certainly never thanked one.

Back in Wisconsin, my life would look more like a street sweeper's than ever: anonymous as a Chinese street cleaner in one of thousands or millions of orange jumpsuits and wide hats, invisible as a driver of a lifeless machine tucked in a box behind dark windows. Where was the art and masterpiece in anonymity, invisibility, bustle and routine? In sending my husband off to work and welcoming him home, in opening Ramen noodle packages and picking up dirty socks, in replying to emails, writing applications and walking the kids again to the neighborhood playground where no one else played, what could possibly make the hosts of heaven and earth pause to notice that?

The idea rustled and rolled with the bouncing of the bus over the cracked highway: How could we be faithful to the brooms, the vacuum cleaners, the paint brushes, web pages, libraries, picket fences, iPads, coffee cups, grocery carts, living rooms and whatever else we've been handed in life? How could we live like life could have ended just today flying from a Kenyan motorcycle, and it could have ended any number of times before or after, but it didn't? How could we live like life is, and always can be, a long stream of Amazing Days?

I described my time in the Kenyan village in an email to Adam, and two days later I received his email back. He had spent the last two weeks at a conference training for his new job in a relatively posh hotel, drinking nice drinks and eating nice eats, sitting and chatting and listening and thinking and "working." In between conference sessions, he wrote, "Very fun and bittersweet to read of your motorcycle ride, coffeemaker/water purifier, cold showers, finding Internet and getting locked out. My experiences have been very different. I have bountiful, timely, healthy meals at the hotel, Wi-Fi *and* 4G, hot showers and water out of the tap."

I noticed that he did not mention any Amazing Days.

■   ■   ■

I decided to open my class in Uganda by sharing as an ice-breaker the story of my high-speed motorcycle race to make it there. The students seemed mildly impressed. After class I sat around a dinner table hearing my students' life stories. One guy's parents lived in Uganda during seven chaotic years of near-constant coups after Uganda's notoriously sadistic ruler, Idi Amin, left power. The student's house was blown up by a rocket-propelled grenade shot by pillaging soldiers when he was eight years old, causing his family to flee the country with another family and their few belongings all jammed into a tiny Daihatsu car. Another man, from Uganda, explained that he alone out of ten children in his family made it past elementary school, and he owed his education to discovering a baby chick caught by a bird of prey in a tree. He had slung a rock at the bird, freed the chick, raised it, sold it for another bird until he had a flock of chickens and thus paid his way through school.

"That's amazing," I said in response to these stories. And they were.

Even if I thought I had something to gain by collecting the most wow stories possible in a lifetime, there would always be somebody who had traveled farther off the beaten path, eaten something weirder, risked a little more, seen a bigger miracle. My years overseas had taught me that a short-term trip with wild motorcycle rides and back-to-back discoveries bore little resemblance to the daily routines and tedious repetitions that shape long-term overseas work even in places that least resemble our homeland. Not every day does a house get blown up, a baby chick fall from a tree or anything exciting happen at all. Living overseas, in its purest sense, had been about seeking the kingdom of God, not seeking dazzling adventures. Now and then those came hand in hand, but in all honesty I knew there was no proven connection between the two. God could appear silently at least as often as he came spectacularly. Like it or not, I had to learn to see and serve God, even while sweeping streets.

3

Faith
Muscles

GETTING MOVING
Chrissy

Months after the trip to Kenya, I lay with my wet cheek smashed against our maroon and yellow quilt. The dishwasher-whacking conversation still clung unsettled in my soul. I stared up at the powder blue bedroom walls that clashed with the quilt, at the maple tree branches swaying outside the window, at the clear blue sky. My watch ticked in my ear as I slowly wadded a piece of toilet paper into a wet lump in my hand.

I hated being weepy. I supposed the weepiness had something to do with too many nights of poor sleep in a row. Lately it was unclear, though, which was the cause and which the effect, whether lack of sleep brought on sadness or sadness cut into sleep. Maybe they both arose from the same cause—a slow stress of nothingness, of guilt that I should be doing more, of not knowing what more to do.

Lying awake between the hours of 1:00 and 4:00 a.m. and in afternoon bouts like this one collapsed on the quilt, I was becoming an expert at producing reasons to doubt myself. I worried that I would forget all about my friends in Africa, that I should be doing more for the billion people on earth living in extreme poverty, that I would not get into a Ph.D. program, that I would become an over-busy working mom, that I would become an under-busy cooped-up mom, that I would never make friends, that my kids would never make friends. I worried that we would all just keep pushing on, pushing on, living our lives in our own fish tanks, day after day, for nothing.

Knowing I should be at my computer writing a speech instead of watching the trees bending in the wind, I worried that someone would find out how wretched I was turning out to be at writing about being amazing, or at really being amazing at all. I had won a big award as a "Distinguished Alumna" from the University of Wisconsin, and on Thursday I was supposed to give a speech on campus for homecoming. I had titled the speech "Amazing Days." Now I just had to write it.

Here I was, a woman who shouts at dishwashers and weeps in the afternoon, trying to inspire people. Writing about being amazing felt a bit like trying to write a how-to book on beating writer's block—a sure set-up for banging your head on a keyboard. I worried that the college students listening would figure out that I was not any more amazing than the next bum. Even if I could fill twenty minutes with "wow stories," they would likely conclude that I was simply a puffed-up, whacked-out volunteer Christian freak on a soapbox. I wanted to be human, to be able to admit right smack down on paper and declare it to an audience that Adam and I were neither the most incredible superhero creatures to ever walk the earth, nor were we as dull as split peas. I felt the competitive commercial world demanding of us the former while everyone I met assumed I was the latter.

In two hours and thirty-six minutes I needed to meet Phoebe and Zeke outside their elementary school to walk them home. Until then, all I wanted to do was give up—give up trying to be inspirational, give up writing, give up caring what happened outside my own cozy little quilt corner.

I lay there trying to think myself back into my college years. What had I learned in college that I wanted to pass along to these students? How had my college years trained me for the years around the world since I graduated?

■   ■   ■

I remembered a phrase from a CD that Adam gave me during my junior year in college, soon after we started dating. The CD was of a local Madison singer named Marques Bovre, who played most weekends at a strange string of venues from bars to the student union to church sanctuaries. On the glossy silver of the CD scrawled in green permanent marker were the words of the album title: "Faith Is a Muscle."

Those words latched on somewhere deep inside me. If faith was a muscle, that meant I had to exercise it. Already my life had been deeply shaped by faith. Since childhood I had learned about Jesus, the Son of God, who forgives our sins and welcomes us into the family of God when we have faith in his death and resurrection as payment for our sins. That all sounds very pat and nice. Before high school I had put my faith in Christ, and as a college freshman I got involved in a Christian student organization that challenged and encouraged my faith. I was learning, as Paul wrote, to "live by faith in the Son of God, who loved me and gave himself for me" (Galatians 2:20).

Paul also wrote in the same verse, "I have been crucified with Christ and I no longer live, but Christ lives in me." While that could sound like a gross zombielike situation of walking around dead under the control of somebody else, or being a big floppy puppet that Christ controls by strings tied to our hands and feet, I knew it meant nothing of the sort. Faith was about letting Christ squelch out all the worthless parts of me—fears, insecurity, pride, all that—and giving Christ a say in everything I did. And then I still had to move.

Exercising my faith muscle became my own little experiment in truth. I stopped trying to pray willy-nilly about stuff I only half cared about to some wishy-washy God who only half cared. Every day I sat in my dormitory room in a big round chair with an open notebook on my lap. I ran through everything I could think of about life. In the front of my notebook I wrote down anything that seemed to need God's work—papers I didn't know how to write, roommates fighting down my hall, minority students feeling prejudice at the university, rain forests getting slashed and burned. Then I asked, *Okay now, if God's doing something about these things, what should I do?* I would flip to the back of my notebook and add on to my list of stuff I needed to do—right that day, that week or sometime in my life.

Sometimes I thought of nothing. Sometimes I listed easy steps like eating lunch with someone or checking out a library book. Other times I listed daunting steps like asking deep probing questions of people I had never met, taking a class that wouldn't count toward graduating or considering careers to have some day. I kept going over my lists and finding items I could check off, which got me all jittery excited to write down more things to pray about and more steps to take. I decided if I was ever going to accomplish half of what was on my list, I was going to have to take this incrementally, practicing as I went, stretching and building my faith muscle in preparation for sprints and marathons. Exercising my faith muscle looked like this: *Listen. Believe. Go. See Christ there. Repeat ad infinitum.*

At the time, my job responsibilities as a residence hall assistant included posting signs on the bulletin board in my dormitory floor's bathroom every week. I pulled the tacks out of old signs, dropped the old signs in the recycling bins and pushed the tacks through new signs. As I tacked, I read the signs. They advertised poetry reads, tuba concerts, workshops in African and Latin dance, Bible studies and Jewish student groups, lectures on subtropical agriculture and stem cell research, engineering study groups, knitting lessons, focus groups on religion and race and gender. I didn't know anyone who attended anything on those signs. I looked at all the things to do, and nobody doing them, and I felt sorry for those signs.

Those signs began providing an endless stream of calisthenics opportunities for my faith muscles. As I read signs, I asked where God might stretch me to go this week. In different ways, I met God where I went. I learned that I loved African dancing and Native American storytelling. I learned to listen thoughtfully to people with whom I expected to disagree. I learned not to be intimidated when, out of a university of over forty thousand students plus thousands of faculty and staff, only I and four other people—three of them professors—showed up at an event. I learned that God made a world full of opportunities and was happy to join me as I tried some.

It certainly helped having as a boyfriend Adam, the guy who rolled down hills for fun and wore two different colored argyle socks. Late one afternoon he dragged me away from studying to share an important discovery: a fire-escape stairway leading all the way from the ground to the roof of a tall building on campus. We looked around nervously for anyone having a look of authority over fire escapes. Finding no one, we climbed it. We sat there with the wind blowing in our hair, gazing out over campus. It might not sound like a very spiritually significant faith exercise to risk sitting on the top of a tile-roofed old building, but God was there. I looked down at all the little students with their backpack hunches slogging to classes and saw I wanted more than that existence. I wanted to be a person who notices a ladder and climbs it. I wanted not to take the same old road every day with my eyes on the ground. I wanted to step aside often enough to remember how the world looks from God's angle.

All this faith exercising prepared me for life overseas. We didn't just one day out of nowhere step onto a plane. We prepared for it, trained for it. From investigating options, to buying plane tickets, to getting up each day in a foreign country and finding something worth doing, the next years were a long trail of *Listen. Believe. Go.*

See God there. Repeat. Those college experiences and a smattering of the overseas adventures that followed could certainly contribute something to an inspirational speech for college students. Now lying on my bed, though, I saw that faith-muscle exercising wasn't just the training I needed for life overseas. My faith-muscles would need just as much exercise back here in the United States.

■　■　■

I sat up in bed, gave my head a few seconds to adjust, threw out my wad of snotty tissue and did something amazing.

I put on my shoes.

Then I drove to the sixty-acre University of Wisconsin arboretum. The summer had been ripe with mosquitoes, but now in the cooler early-autumn weather their numbers were down. The forest exuded a lush smell of wet leaves. Tiny white and yellow flowers peeked out in sunny patches beneath the trees.

Faith exercising, like any exercise, always sounds least appealing when you're stuck in the inertia of lying on a bed or repeating the same routine every day. Already now as my feet crunched through leaves, I felt the freedom of breaking that inertia. I remembered a quote from our peace activist, community-living, seventy-year-old friend Don Mosley: "You don't think your way into new ways of acting. You act your way into new ways of thinking."

I had seen the same inertia-breaking work in my children. One spring Saturday earlier that year during our first months back in the United States, Adam and I had dawdled at our computers answering emails and editing photos for the first half of the morning while the children stewed, annoying each other with little hums and sound effects as they fought for couch space. Finally Adam stood up, stretched his shoulders and announced, "Let's go for a walk."

Phoebe moaned and slid off the couch like a spoonful of jam. Dropping the book she had been reading, she whined, "Do we have to?"

Fifteen minutes later, Phoebe in her thrift-store baby blue spring jacket and Zeke in his favorite scuffed brown boots charged ahead on a woodsy trail near our home, playing a freshly invented game called "Toss the stick." Adam slipped his fingers through mine. Phoebe stopped to pick a dried flower of Queen Anne's Lace, looked up and said with a dimpled smile, "I love this place."

Farther along the path we found a fallen tree. The kids climbed up and clung to the branches for dear life, rocking and rolling in shrieks of giggles while Adam and I took turns jumping on the opposite end of the tree like a teeter-totter catapult. Phoebe shouted between giggles, "It's like a ride at the fair!"

That was the highest compliment I could imagine Phoebe giving an activity. To her, the fair was a mythical place, something she had read about in books but never experienced during her life overseas. The fair was something you wait for, pay lots of money for, only get to try one or two rides at, but live for all year long. And here, on a free walk in the woods on a weekday afternoon, throwing away fears of our children crashing down four feet from a rotten tree branch to a dirt path, we had stumbled upon all the joy of a fair. I could have reminded her—but knew better than to tell her—that she had not wanted to leave the couch.

Now as I walked through the arboretum, I wondered why we adults still find it so difficult to get moving in life. Whenever I looked back over my lists of prayers from past years, I would always find requests that remained unanswered for years. Did God just forget these prayers? What about that famous Bible verse about "ask and it will be given to you; seek and you will find" (Matthew 7:7)? I found it hard to believe that God would leave people in such stagnant waters for so long without a single opportunity to move toward the good dreams people claimed to most desire. I knew people with all the skills and ambitions to start their own businesses, who never worked up the courage to begin. I knew people who left church over some spat and meant to find a new one but never tried for so long that they could scarcely remember what it felt like to get out of bed before ten o'clock on a Sunday morning. I knew people nursing grudges, wishing for a spouse, growing disillusioned with their career paths. In my own life I saw goals that seemed so huge that I had defaulted to doing nothing. I wondered how many times people missed on-ramps to a better future because they did not really ask and seek, or because they didn't like what they heard and found. Sometimes the road God leads us on looks steep or overgrown. We worry that we'll get lost or pricked or dirty or pass some *No Trespassing* sign, when really the path is waiting to be enjoyed.

■   ■   ■

After college as my faith exercising continued into our first year overseas, I met an old Nicaraguan woman named Yaya who was an expert in the art of trespassing. Yaya had the appearance of the granny in the old Tweety Bird cartoons, a slightly stooped wrinkled woman who sometimes chose not to wear the false teeth she had saved much of a year's wages to purchase. She was a widow whose children had all moved away to find work, leaving behind her three grandchildren essentially as orphans in her care. The children spent more time with her in their corn and bean fields than at school, and food was scarce. They often invited me to spend afternoons at their home sharing stories over a cup of coffee they had grown, harvested and roasted. One day they invited me to join them on a journey down the mountain where we lived to visit a nearby plantation.

We left at dawn, sliding down the steep mountain trail, catching ourselves on branches and hoisting each other over fallen logs into the coffee and banana plantation owned by a wealthy landlord. There, Yaya and her three children taught me to find fallen bananas that were too ripe for the landlord to sell. We topped off our sacks with large round mangolike fruits called *mamei* that dropped from seventy-foot trees along the roadside. We were tropical elves, carrying home sacks of delicious presents, laughing along the way.

As we carried home the fruit of our gleanings, Yaya spotted ahead on the road the gun-carrying guard of the plantation. "*Apúrate, Cristina!* Hurry!" she urged as we skirted onto a side road behind a cornfield to hide. Only then did I realize that what they were doing would be considered stealing from the plantation owner.

Yaya teaches Chrissy to roast coffee.

We saw just how risky Yaya's trips were months later, when Adam and a friend revisited the plantation. Security guards picked them up for trespassing and turned them over to police for a night in a Nicaraguan jail. After tedious paperwork including questions like, "So what do you like to eat in the United States?" the police decided to let them go. Adam and our friend spent a poor night of sleep in the jail's flea-infested beds before they could catch a bus back home up the mountain the next day, but we never knew whether Yaya would have gotten off as easily as the two foreigners.

Yaya never seemed the least bit ashamed about teaching us to trespass. She carried out the work so innocently, purely confident that as a widow with orphans in her care she fully deserved the fruit that would rot on the ground. She knew that fruit would nourish her hungry grandchildren. So she went and got it.

■   ■   ■

As I wandered from trail to trail in the arboretum, I wondered how often people don't get the very thing they need. Maybe in going too long without nature or community or meaningful activity, people gum up their nerve endings. I wondered what other need-sensors had been buzzing at me lately that I chose not to listen to. Perhaps the loneliness I felt lately was not such a bad thing, but a good reminder that something important in me could still be resuscitated from near death.

I remembered an afternoon when Zeke had come penguin-walking out from the room where he was supposed to be napping. He cautiously waddled up to my desk, knowing full well that he should be asleep, and blinked his big eyes up at my face. "It feels like I need to be outside."

I set him on my lap and asked what made him feel that way.

"It just smells like it," he said.

Perhaps today some internal smelling sensor had been telling me the same thing and I had been ignoring it.

Tired of swatting bugs, I headed for a break in the trees where a boardwalk cut through a spread of cattails and swamp grass. At the end of the boardwalk, quietly tucked away, was a covered shelter on stilts above the water with benches lining the edges. The mosquitoes here above the swamp were surprisingly few, deterred by the bright sunlight. A bird let out an intermittent little *tweet* from the trees behind me as if to keep me company. Insects buzzed a monotonous drone and the cattails and marsh grasses waved softly in the breeze. After a while, a lone frog began chirruping calmly from somewhere beneath the shelter.

I stretched my legs out along the wood bench with my toes in the sunlight and pulled out the book I had thrown into my purse as I left home. The book, *Thoughts in Solitude*, by a monk named Thomas Merton, was due back to the library soon, and I had yet to read past the first page. Now in the still hum of nature, my ears were opened to every word as they flowed over me like the wind across the grasses.

> Sooner or later if we follow Christ we have to risk everything in order to gain everything. We have to gamble on the invisible and risk all that we can see and taste and feel. But we know the risk is worth it.[3]

Compared to my past years living in a mountaintop village with no cell phones or health care, traipsing through the forest with Yaya, or even being a Christian college student who showed up at meetings of the atheists' campus group or listened to homeless people, today didn't seem to involve taking much risk at all. What had I really accomplished today by heading out into the arboretum? Was it risky? Amazing? Maybe not on the surface, but I had risked feeling dumb, coming back more discouraged than ever and wasting time. The risks of looking dumb and of wasting time might not seem like big risks, but they sure stop people from doing a lot of things. It takes faith to trust God doesn't waste our time.

I began scribbling notes in the tiny notebook I kept in my purse, page after page of quotes giving answers to the doubts and worries I had felt.

Without courage we can never attain to true simplicity. Cowardice keeps us "double-minded"—hesitating between the world and God. In this hesitation, there is no true faith—faith remains an opinion. We are never certain, because we never quite give in to the authority of an invisible God. This hesitation is the death of hope. We never let go of those visible supports which, we well know, must one day surely fail us. And this hesitation makes true prayer impossible—*it never quite dares to ask for anything.*[4]

Cowardice. I underlined the word. Was it cowardice that kept me stuck lying on my bed? At some deep psychological level, I had equated life in middle-class United States with cowardice. Middle-class suburbanite Americans, I judged, didn't do much of anything that required faith like Merton talked about, the kind of faith that takes off visible supports and isn't just an opinion. The kind of faith that puts on shoes. At a superficial, be-nice level, I knew that every believer was just as important in the kingdom of God, and God didn't think that world-traveling missionaries were automatically better people than web designers and basketball coaches in U.S. suburbs and small towns. A part of me was saying that while believing something else, though. An ugly deep piece of me believed this was a place of cowards, and now that meant me too. That was a lie, and not a nice one at all—toxic to my neighbors, destructive to me, evil toward God. In believing that lie, I was giving myself no way out. I had expected nothing more of myself than to get sucked into the vortex of the cowardly do-nothing existence I assumed everyone else was in. Expecting to fail had paved a highway to failure.

I looked back over what I had copied and underlined more words. *Courage. Faith. Real prayer. Dare.* These were the way out of the lie. I didn't have to be the boring, faithless coward that I feared. I could expect more of myself, more of my neighbors and more of God, even here. I set the Thomas Merton book upside down on the bench next to me and flipped over a new page in my notebook. I began to make a new list: tasks I had known I needed to do for months, new ideas, crazy ideas, ideas for starting some routines and stopping others.

I felt some sadness that there was not more spontaneity about checking off items from a list, but there was a realism in my list of goals that felt enormously comforting. I was past expecting myself to just wake up in the morning full of pep to go talk to a homeless lady and write a brilliant blog post about it. If my few weeks thus far as a full-time stay-at-home writer had taught me anything, it was that spontaneity is an undependable racecar to drive: now and then you get the ride of your life. More often you sit by the roadside poorly equipped, bored and bitter. I was not a superhero naturally inclined to go out and *carpe* every *diem*. Some *diems* I wouldn't feel like *carpe*-ing. I had to somehow ask God what mattered, offer it up to God and then go do something about it. That would require a well-exercised faith muscle.

■   ■   ■

I often think of time as a bulldozer, shoving us along with the mountains of tasks we try to accomplish. As the time bulldozer pushes, tasks drop off to the sides, leaving a trail of what might have been if only we could have managed more, kept it all piled tightly together. We generally live as if we are at the mercy of the bulldozer. Items fall off our to-do list after weeks pass without making them a high enough priority. Emails slide to the bottom of our inbox until we're too embarrassed at the tardiness to reply to them. And so life goes, pushed by an enormous inexorable machine steered by a faceless, heartless driver.

Today, though, I remembered a different image of a bulldozer from another walk. Earlier in the year the kids and I came outside to find a sky of puffy white clouds and perfect T-shirt temperature. Phoebe strapped on her old hand-me-down, white, Styrofoam-marshmallow bike helmet, and Zeke sat on his bike balanced over the training wheels with the perfect posture of a secretary bird. They both began to pedal.

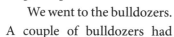

Phoebe delights in the bulldozer "playground."

We went to the bulldozers. A couple of bulldozers had been parked along the edge of our trailer park long enough to sink six inches deep in solid soil. It seemed no one had disturbed or noticed the machines for years, except my children, who often choose this spot over the nearby playground. I sat on the rusted mud-caked tread, not caring about the dirt on my jeans, letting the children climb far higher than my head. Phoebe stood on the engine holding the exhaust pipe, talking to the tree and scolding it for catching her hair with a branch. Zeke yanked the handles, fully convinced he was in charge of doing some serious damage with his rig.

Maybe my kids weren't really controlling the machine. So what? To them the bulldozer was a great discovery, a free playground, a ladder to the sky. Watching my children waving sticks and shouting like warriors conquering the bulldozer, I remembered that we are not just victims of the bulldozer of time. We're not just sitting on a stalled-out bulldozer, nor are we doomed to slide in the rubble in front of the blade until we too fall off some edge and time for us is done. We get to make choices. We get to set goals. We get to pray. We get to participate in a world where God is in charge. We get to live by faith.

Faith cleans us up. It tells us to throw away that tissue wad and go open the door to the friend inviting you to the rooftops, or to the widowed grandma taking you out trespassing for rotten bananas. Faith invites, enables, finds the bridge across the chasm. And then we have to walk it. *Listen. Believe. Go. See God there. Repeat.* Every day, every year. As long as life endures.

I picked up the Merton book again and read, "Life reveals itself to us only in so far as we live it. . . . Life is not attained by reasoning and analysis, but first of all by living."[5]

ORDINARY ADVENTURES
to Exercise Your Faith Muscles

- Pray for the length of time it takes to finish a hot beverage.
- Eat lunch in a park.
- Pick up litter.
- Email your friends and ask for prayer requests.
- Sit quietly in a church alone.
- Climb a fire escape or a mountain.
- Get mud on your shoes . . . and jeans and shirt.
- Write a poem outside.
- Watch a bulldozer at work (or ask to drive it).

4

THORNS
AND THISTLES

WORK
Adam

While Chrissy was out playing on bulldozers and walking in the arboretum, I was finding and starting my first eight-to-five office job (which is never just eight-to-five, so whatever).

For years, I'd had unorthodox work situations:

- baking hundreds of loaves of bread each week
- teaching ESL in three countries
- laboring on a farm
- marketing coffee
- working as a camp counselor
- translating in hospitals
- being a residence hall director
- directing a microfinance project
- teaching on leadership
- leading communications for a small seminary

None of these jobs consisted of regular or typical hours. Most of them were shared or split with Chrissy. All were flexible, enabling me to watch Phoebe and Zeke as needed. My work changed frequently (along with the continent on which I worked).

All this ground to a halt as I rode off on my bike for my first routine office job.

On my first day, I got there early, took a lunch break with new coworkers, worked dutifully until five and rode home. I was away for about nine-and-a-half hours, one small part of a big organization spread across the whole country. I wore a tie to score some professionalism points (and to remind myself that I was working).

This new job was with InterVarsity Christian Fellowship, a large nonprofit campus ministry. I was to lead a team of writers who tell the story of what God is doing through the organization on over five hundred campuses. We lead conversations on our national social media, organize people to pray, ask people and foundations for donations, thank people who give, keep up on what people are saying about the organization, and produce tools for ministry on campus so that more people can share and live their Christian faith well.

I also serve on the leadership team for the Urbana Student Missions Conference, an event we hold every three years, challenging people to give their whole lives for God's global mission. And I'm on an advisory group on partnership for InterVarsity and World Vision. I work closely with teams on design, video and web projects too. This work has me at the table with very intelligent, creative, passionate, fun, faithful people. It's a really cool job.

But right away when I started, I noticed that our office culture wasn't quite as interesting or fun a workplace as I'd expected. I pictured Googleishness—whiteboards, overstuffed chairs, tidal waves of creativity and cool socks. Instead, we sat in cubicles. Our voices were hushed. Keyboards clicked and heads were down. If that's how things were going to be, I wasn't going to last long. So I took matters into my own hands at the end of my first week. I called my creative colleagues together for a special meeting.

"Thank you for joining me today," I announced. "In my first week in the office, it's come to my attention that we don't have many elegant gelatin desserts here. In fact, I have yet to see a single gelatin dessert here in the office. I aim to remedy that." People looked around at each other. *What the heck is going on?* they wondered, nervously trying to smile.

"Behold, the crown jewel of Jell-O!" I unveiled and lifted high a platter of solidified pink goo with sparkling cubes embedded in it, garnished, of course, with dollops of Cool Whip.

As we scooped up the Jell-O, I pushed the event one step further.

Another of Adam's fabulous Jell-O creations lightens a workday.

"Now, surely we all have fond memories of Jell-O dishes and occasions from our youth, from our families, from last week. Let's go around the room and each share just one—*please, just one*—story about how Jell-O has had a positive impact on your life, creating a pleasant memory." Asking this of a team of people I had only just met felt a bit risky, with the serious possibility of crashing and burning.

Tick. Tick. Tick. Feet shuffled. Throats swallowed. Eyeballs bored into the floor. I looked around, making eye contact with two of the fifteen people. They quickly looked away, perhaps fearing I would call on them. I took in a deep breath ready to explain again that maybe in eating the delicious Jell-O treat together, we would get more comfortable with one another, or that perhaps people would begin sharing in small groups.

Jill spoke up. "My grandma always used to make a green one with carrots in it. And she served it on a lettuce leaf with a little dollop of Miracle Whip. It was a little weird but also a nice tradition. We still do it."

Next Donna shared how she hosted her first large family gathering after getting married. "When I was carrying the last dish to the table for our Easter dinner, a purple and yellow Jell-O mold, I tripped! Jell-O flew through the air, landed in the middle of the white table cloth, bounced, split apart and splattered the room! I've never lived it down."

Gary chimed in, "My older brother would make Jell-O for a singles group he went to—raspberry with Cool Whip and walnuts on top. Sometimes we'd get a bit too. We thought that was pretty smart. Who wouldn't want to date someone that could make such great Jell-O?"

And Christy chipped in with how her mom would make her lime Jell-O whenever she was sick. "To this day, green Jigglers are kind of comforting."

And so we went around the group, talking for fifteen minutes about our memories of gelatin desserts. I couldn't believe it. I had stepped out to do something that's a little bit odd, to break up the ordinary. I didn't really have time to make a Jell-O that week. And I know that most of my coworkers didn't really have time to stand around chatting about the crown jewel Jell-O dessert and our best memories of other elegant gelatin. But since work takes up the bulk of our time and work can sometimes get a bit dull, we were all willing to spend some time doing something together, even if a bit corny. Maybe we didn't have a workspace like Google's, but as the new guy, I really appreciated other people joining in some fun. And I think it was the first in many steps toward a stronger team and even better working friendships. I figured I was in a good place.

They even paid me at the end of the month.

■   ■   ■

Eventually, of course, the job-love honeymoon ended. The hours got longer. I had a hard time figuring out budget issues for my team. I grasped for ideas on how we could do better, struggling to really see and understand the various pieces of content we put out, often too swamped by urgent emails to step out into a wider view of how to do our work better. I tried to plan, but my good intentions still often left us scrambling to edit and proofread at the eleventh hour. I felt like I should be running at full speed, telling stories of how Jesus was affecting students' lives on campus. Instead, it was like running in quicksand.

Then one day, a coworker in leadership took me aside with some concerns about the work I was doing and how I was doing it. I knew the issue wasn't just the Jell-O. "You're the new guy. It's good to ask questions and be curious. It's good to offer your outsider perspective. But you need to be careful how you do that. You need to understand the culture and history here. You need to be conscious of the 'political landscape' of the office. People won't like it if you don't listen well and want to change too much too fast."

At that, I started to see spots, and the whole room zoomed away from me. I felt dizzy. I took a deep breath. I shook my head.

I don't know how the conversation ended or what else was said. I was hung up at "political landscape." I might have walked out in the middle of my coworker's next sentence. I might have mumbled some thanks and, "Back to the grind, eh?"

I should have known better. Any group of people (even with a clear vision and purpose, with shared values, even with a doctrinal basis) has a "political landscape." We are supposed to be on the same team, with the same Captain. But our own preferences, opinions and interpretations keep us from getting things done effectively. I'm not exempt from this. I was taken aback when it was mentioned, but as I drove home that day, I had to admit that I'd wanted to know and navigate and maybe even play my own part in the political landscape, though I'd not called it that.

And once I acknowledged that, sitting in traffic on the highway home, I thought of thorns, thistles and sweat.

■   ■   ■

In the Bible, God said to Adam, after he and Eve had just messed up big time: "Cursed is the ground because of you; through painful toil you will eat food from it all the days of your life. It will produce thorns and thistles for you, and you will eat the plants of the field. By the sweat of your brow you will eat your food" (Genesis 3:17-19).

This names a primary consequence of sin, a characteristic of God's judgment. Work existed before sin—God had Adam and Eve caring for and harvesting from the garden. But due to sin, we can expect our labor to be hard, our sweat to be profuse, our tasks to be frustrating.

Over the years, Chrissy and I became experts on thorns and thistles through our gardening attempts. When we lived in South Africa, the high school and seminary students we worked with had the month off, and we had the opportunity to travel back to the

Adam helps Zeke tackle weeds in our South African garden.

United States to visit family and friends. December happens to hit in the middle of the South African summer. Every year, Chrissy planted a garden, and every year we came back to shoulder-high weeds. One time when we arrived home Zeke yelled, "Our garden is crazy!" And it was. Grassy weeds grew higher than my bellybutton. I let out a sigh. "This is going to take a lot of work."

We certainly did sweat and toil to preserve any chance of eating peppers, tomatoes or squash. We fought against the vicious, chaotic inner tendency or entropy that naturally throws up weeds and pests and disease. Work is hard. This is true in the garden, and this is true in the office.

But we toil anyway.

It shouldn't surprise me when my job ends up pushing on good parts of life, constricting that which ought to grow and flourish. Even when I have cut down all the thorns and thistles I can, there are still more than I can really cope with. They grow really fast.

■   ■   ■

As my weeks on the job skidded past, my meetings got more frequent, my task list got longer, and my bike rides were often replaced with driving to carve out a few extra minutes. My arrivals were earlier, and my departures sometimes slid later. I would call Chrissy to apologize for another late night while I skimmed through some of the six hundred emails clogging my inbox after one week out of the office. I was working in communications, but this level of communication was going to kill me.

I try to avoid being dead weight around the house. My goal was to cook a couple nights a week, to do the dishes whenever I didn't cook and to clean something once in a while. I was also working on a Master of Theology degree through a distance education program, which I'd started back in South Africa. Plus we kept trying to live a generous, involved life, with the local church as the basis for that, so we started volunteering as greeters and Sunday school teachers at a new church called The Vine. And I still photographed the occasional wedding and continued to take on some freelance writing projects. I had already given up almost all of my personal reading time and I only watched a couple TV shows or a movie in a week's time.

Meanwhile, the kids looked forward to playing games and reading books with me. They wanted me to play Twister, Dinosaurs Extinct?, and Chutes and Ladders. Phoebe wanted me to read her the Narnia series, and Zeke asked me to guide him through *The Adventurous Boy's Handbook*. I loved doing all this stuff, but all the fun and learning got squeezed. Some nights we only had about fifteen minutes together after dinner and dishes.

Fifteen minutes? This was not the family dynamic I signed up for. What happened to the calm afternoons of walks and chopping vegetables for slow long meals we enjoyed in South Africa? Was there any way to replicate our annual six-week trip back to the U.S. to visit family and friends? During the years we lived in South Africa we came back around Christmas each year to see family and friends, to rest and to do some fundraising, and to celebrate Thanksgiving and Christmas. We had great times as a family as we traveled about, reconnecting to our homeland. Were those weeks together now destined to be just memories?

Would we ever have slow meals with friends again? What about all the meaningful conversations Chrissy had with women while making tortillas or with our Chinese students as we strolled outside the campus? Why didn't people have tea times like in South Africa? Could I ever be as close to Phoebe and Zeke as I'd been abroad, or was I now doomed to showing up late to Little League still wearing my loosened tie?

I was ready to take a machete and hack down some of the thistles that were hemming me in.

■   ■   ■

Chrissy and I got a babysitter for the kids and went for a walk around our neighborhood one day. "There are too many plates spinning," I said. "But what am I going to drop? Work is work. Family is family. I think it's our responsibility to serve through the church. I can't imagine not carrying on with my writing and photography . . ." I kicked a stone down the sidewalk.

Chrissy stepped out on a limb: "What would happen if you dropped your master's program?"

I blew out a deep breath, squeezed my lips to one side, and looked up at the maples and elms along the side of the street. I hadn't quit much of anything since I dropped out of debate in high school. Quitting my M.Th. program would mean accepting that there are limits on my career path (and life). I don't like admitting that. I would not be getting theological training that I wanted. I would not be researching how nonprofits use images in their publicity materials and how that honors (or doesn't) the people they serve, a topic I find fascinating. The program felt like an important training opportunity, keeping me sharp in academics, helping me become an expert in something. I had a good deal of my identity wrapped up in it.

And I don't think I'm alone.

In the U.S. when we introduce ourselves, we usually talk about what we do during our working hours. It's a shorthand for what kind of person you are—I say I work in communications, and they rightfully assume I type on a Mac and like whiteboards. I say it's for a nonprofit and they think I'm driven by values more than dollars—right again. We all have images and assumptions that come to mind when someone mentions any of these job titles:

- engineer
- bus driver
- sales clerk at Sears
- stripper
- plumber
- lawyer
- stay-at-home mom
- waiter
- realtor

Like it or not, we have our stereotypes, and to various degrees we embrace or distance ourselves from the one we think people have of us, of our position. We do this to craft our identity—we want to be a certain kind of person and we want others to know it (or at least think it).

This colors how we define *amazing*, as well as *worthwhile, important, generous, interesting* and more. And that determines what we seek, what we post on Facebook, how we live. We measure ourselves and others by categories ranging from income bracket to advanced degrees to hobbies to gadgets to impact on society to followers on Twitter to high-achieving kids. For me, the pursuit of a master's in theology was tied up in wanting to love God and to consider practical theology more carefully, but it was also connected to proving myself, to showing that I matter, to gaining power.

"Something's got to give," I admitted. "I don't want to drop it, but I don't see any way around it."

And just like that I was no longer a student. I am only one person, and no matter how much I might fight it, I can't do everything I want to do. In choosing one career path, I unchoose countless others. I have a lot of good ideas, I enjoy learning, and I could do some great work in a lot of different roles. To do anything meaningful in any of those roles, though, I need to focus and focus and refocus. In the process, I have to say no to things because time presses in on me. I am coping.

■   ■   ■

In working with InterVarsity, I had the opportunity to attend the World Assembly of the International Fellowship of Evangelical Students (IFES) in Krakow, Poland. There, I sat with a group of people from eight different countries. We read John 12:20-36, which includes, "Unless a kernel of wheat falls to the ground and dies, it remains only a single seed. But if it dies, it produces many seeds. Anyone who loves their life will lose it, while anyone who hates their life in this world will keep it for eternal life" (vv. 24-25).

We talked around the table about our homelands—Croatia, Belgium, Zimbabwe, Serbia, Australia and two countries that cannot be mentioned because of security concerns. Together, we considered what it means for Christians today to "hate our lives," to give them up to "take up our crosses" and follow a king who was killed on his.

The conversation went around. "It's giving up the superficial and materialistic," the woman from Croatia said. The leader from Zimbabwe stared down at his hands and said, "It's getting kicked out of your church for a desire to live out what you read in the Bible." "It's not being very secret despite real dangers, but loving neighbors in visible, tangible ways," said the woman from one of the countries whose name I can't include.

And then the young woman with wide, fierce eyes, from the other dangerous country, began in halting English.

Carrying the cross like Jesus is hard. When they arrested me and my husband, we [were] separated by them. The man teased, "There is no problem with your faith, maybe you had a dream or something and you are confused. The problem is why you share that news with other peoples? You say, 'Okay, I don't share Jesus anymore.' Why don't you say it? Then I let you go, free."

At that time, God say to me, "If you don't want to share this good news, if you don't want to tell others about Jesus, you are not following me."

Yesterday, I visited Auschwitz. It was horrible. Many die. I think of my friend—he's in jail. Eight months.

God say to me, "When you have problem because friends are in cell, in a bad situation, I never leave you."

When students in my country come to Christ, they know they will have problems. They will go to jail. They stand and follow Jesus. They know one day they will get a knock on their door.

They will go to jail. But they still follow. They still tell others.

God gives us power. There is a verse in the Bible about standing before the judges and do not worry what you say because the Spirit will tell you what to say. I know God cares for me in every hard situation. He will do work for me. People's hearts are soft. We have a problem. But God helps us.

Jail for women is terrible in my country. Nobody ever knows anything. It is a big fight in your mind. But we know God is with us every day, more in jail than outside.

When I was arrested, that man also say to me, "You know when I release you, no one will talk to you. They know the danger of you now, of talking to you now. You are now like death to them."

I let out a shallow breath and fought back tears as I realized the jailer had it exactly inside out—she was *life* to her friends, including me. She was offering good news, hope and freedom despite the dangers. She carries on with her work despite some very big thorns. She has learned to pray, to regard her life and work rightly.

This dear sister believes the God who says, "If you remain in me and my words remain in you, ask whatever you wish, and it will be done for you" (John 15:7). She trusts the One who "in all things . . . works for the good of those who love him" (Romans 8:28).

Now that I'm back in the U.S., when I face my own little problems, I want to respond in the same way this brave woman does. I want her courage and devotion. And when I take the time to step back and glance around at my life, I see that God has wrought some good in me as I deal with the thorns and thistles of work. I cannot complain.

I've also learned that when my work is hard, I need to ask why. Sometimes the struggles that keep me from working well have been my self-generated internal issues—fear, ego or greed. When that's the case, I have to get honest with myself (and God).

■   ■   ■

I need to wake up early. In college, I was usually up by about 7:00. I'd typically grab my Bible and a notebook and head to the basement of Cole Hall. There was never a soul down there, so I had a big room in which I could pace, read (aloud when I wanted), write, memorize passages of the Bible that I wanted to chew on and pray as long as I needed, to muster strength for the day. I did the same with a plastic cup of steaming sweet black coffee in my hand while the sun rose above distant volcanic peaks in Nicaragua. In China I walked past the *niu rou mian* shops to the banks of the Yellow River. In South Africa I drank endless cups of proper tea with milk while I looked out over a foggy field and let the Bible echo through my head.

This pattern has served me very well in dealing with my frustrations at work back here in the U.S. too. There's an expectation among certain Christian groups that we're all reading the Bible and praying daily. I'm far from perfectly consistent in these disciplines. But when I'm put through the wringer by the office's "political landscape," or whatever the crisis or disappointment du jour, I find that I am much more faithful in spending some time in the morning reading a bit of that Good Book and sitting before my Father, telling him how tired I am, how frustrated I am, how I need help, how I wish he'd smite so-and-so. He never seems to smite anyone for me, but he does give me peace that I don't understand, as well as gumption to take another crack at a new day.

The more I struggle internally, the more I need to get up early and sigh and pace and pray. I am often reminded how much I have yet to learn in this area when I hear from sisters and brothers in the church around the world whose struggles seem so exponentially larger than mine.

Sometimes, the battle is outside of myself and deals with actual tasks, situations and people that make the work difficult. In these cases, I need to look for a new way to deal with the work and the struggle. Failing that, it's time to find other work. In either case, from now on I'm going to try to remember the stunningly simple wisdom of my friend: "God is with us every day." I need to find the ultimate in the difficult, no matter how tall the thorns and thistles might grow.

■   ■   ■

Sometimes, though, I just need to suck it up.

We lived and taught in Lanzhou, the most polluted city in the world, when we moved there in 2003. There were heavy industrial factories, sandstorms and a ring of mountains that kept the air thick year-round. Lanzhou is the capital of Gansu province in northwest China, sort of a backwater, forgotten part of the country.

We taught at Lanzhou Shi Zhuan, a teacher-training college. Our students would finish their degrees and head back to villages around Gansu province to teach in the schools. Most wished they had gotten into Xi Bei Shi Da, the larger and more prestigious institution down the road. But they knew this college was better than nothing. They worked hard to make it this far, many coming from remote villages where even high schools were few and far between. These kids knew how to work.

They got up for mandatory morning exercises at 6:45, ate a breakfast of spicy beef noodle soup or fried dough and soy milk, hit their classrooms at 8:00 for the morning lectures, then had lunch, then attended more classes and studied until 4:00, took a walk with a friend or played some Ping-Pong before dinner, and then studied in their classroom again from 6:30 until 11:00. They wrote and re-wrote essays. And on top of this, the Chinese system takes off time for fewer holidays than we do in the U.S.

So when I feel a fit of whining coming on because I have to work ten hours one day or have to spend some time messing around with software I find tedious or need to deal with some public criticism, I think back to the most dedicated of our students who had the self-control and discipline to keep this routine up, even in the long, dark, cold, polluted winter months, all in hopes of getting one of the teaching jobs.

Beyond these students on the other side of the planet, I can also point to an example across town that challenges me to regard work rightly.

■   ■   ■

For the last year and a half, my friend Nate has worked half-time at Starbucks. The other half of his time, he's one of our pastors at The Vine, the upstart church we attend. Being a pastor has its own challenges—learning to properly care for people, feeling responsible for people's faith and growth, and experiencing pressure on family responsibilities. I see Nate at church and at leadership meetings, working out solutions to these challenges with the other two pastors.

But I've also been able to watch as Nate searched for a part-time job with health insurance that would allow him to be near the University of Wisconsin campus because he wants to help students meet and follow Jesus. Nate gets up really early to sling lattes at undergrads before they're awake. He deals with crazy rushes, with lines snaking to the door, with loud conversations blathering around him, with sore feet as he dances around calling out orders. Nate has chosen this path to get insurance, yes, but his primary drive is to share the love of Christ with people he works around, to answer hard questions of faith, to model a different way of living and a healthy family life. Nate never dreamed of working at Starbucks as the fulfillment of some longtime aspiration. But he's willing to because he loves Jesus and he loves other people. God's got him handing out scones, so he does it excellently, just like the street sweeper in the MLK quote that Chrissy heard from Mike in Kenya.

In the U.S., I find it really easy to manufacture a lot of challenges. I make myself busy. I bite off more than I can chew. I fail to set limits. And then I continually find myself thinking and saying that someday I'm going to get through it (whatever "it" is, whether college, Nicaragua, grad school, the kids being in diapers or the job hunt), popping out of the other side of my busyness. I'll finally find "free" time, an open schedule, no piddly tasks eating up my minutes and hours. I'll get to finally indulge in all the time-wasting pleasure I want.

But that never comes—it's the North American myth. We do get moments or days of rest, but there is always more to do. And that's *good*—"We are God's handiwork, created in Christ Jesus to do good works, which God prepared in advance for us to do" (Ephesians 2:10). But in the midst of all the good stuff we get to be a part of, we need to remain centered. Rather than just accept what's normal, I want to press to match up better with Jesus' abnormality.

I can throw myself a pity party just about every day—some project is stalled, I had to have a hard conversation with someone I supervise, I feel tired, my computer punked out, the hits on the blog are down, somebody blew up over something somewhere in the country and now they're spewing half-truths about InterVarsity and I need to reply with truth *and* love.

Despite all the thorns and thistles, I know I need to keep tilling the soil, caring for sprouting seeds and watering the dry spots. I need to remember my courageous sister overseas,

A common South African sight: the thorns of an acacia tree.

my best Chinese students and my friend Nate. And when I harvest wheat, there will be a good harvest, even if it's speckled with a few weeds.

ORDINARY ADVENTURES
at Work

- Start a lunch discussion group on a topic.
- Move a meeting outside.
- Make Jell-O.
- Hold a watermelon-seed-spitting contest at work.
- Send thank you cards to your coworkers.
- Start a squirt gun fight.
- Go in very early one day.
- Do all your least favorite work on one day.
- Find out how much you'd be paid if you had your same job in a developing country.

5

The Cool
Table

IDENTITY
Chrissy

hat's a great accomplishment, writing a book," a friend marveled while at a gathering of old friends from college. Our family had
spent the previous month driving through a dozen states on a book
tour for my first book. Now we were back in Wisconsin with old
friends, catching up on ages of each other's children, new career
paths, struggles and accomplishments since the last time we had
seen each other a year ago. From our lawn chairs lined up near the
grill, we took turns reminding our children not to ride their scooters
into the street, not to pour dirt in their shoes, not to throw basket-
balls at the toddlers. Fluff floated down from a neighbor's cottonwood
tree like a dreamy magical snowfall through seventy-five-degree
spring weather.

Not everyone in the group brought stories of wild adventures or
great accomplishments. Someone hated her boss and wanted a new
job. Someone was still single and sick of churches with meat market
singles groups. Someone had tried for years to have kids and felt life
was at a standstill. Someone's marriage was going cold. Someone

was on a third university degree and still wondering if he would ever find a job that fit. Around the circle, new bulging muffin-top bellies and gray hairs appeared. The cracks in our dreams were showing.

"It's like you've created something eternal," another college friend admired. "After you die," he said, "that book will still be there. Just think of it, there on library shelves for people you've never even met to just pick it up and read it."

I could eat up people's compli- ments like candy, but I knew as

Feeling famous, Chrissy earns an alumni award and gets a ride in the University of Wisconsin homecoming parade.

soon as my candy ran out I would be the forlorn little girl holding her empty plastic pumpkin candy bucket crying for another Halloween to come.

Even as I sat wondering how to respond to compliments on my first book, half my brain scrutinized the little girls and boys in our gathering, measuring up my children. Phoebe was scooping out dandelions and transplanting them into a patch of dirt under a bush. Zeke was flying on his belly on a swing. The conversation drifted to stories about the soccer and basketball clubs these friends' children were attending each week. Comparing their training regimens to the void of sports our children had practiced in their South African upbringing, I wondered if I'd already condemned my children to being the last ones picked for the baseball team for the rest of their lives and retreating to playground fringes to transplant weeds.

■   ■   ■

I had plenty of other worries of how I would measure up. I was applying for Ph.D. programs at big universities, which meant I had the GRE test to take, applications to fill out, and years of academic rigor and publishing (or perishing) to follow.

The day I took the GRE exam, I left the silent computer cubicle repeating the scores that had flashed on the screen, drilling them into my stupefied brain to scribble down when I reached my car and look up when I returned home. All the way home my numb brain asked the same question: *Was I good enough?* At home I compared the scores to percentile rankings and average scores for others admitted into my Ph.D. program of preference. Were they good enough? Maybe. They sat right on the bottom edge of what I had hoped to score. I would have to wait another six months before results came in from my graduate school and funding applications. In the meantime I would keep playing the game. I would lay my life under the scrutiny of an invisible courtroom of judges, talk to potential advisers, clean up my resumé, sharpen the wording for my application, and repeat the story of my credentials, my experience and my life accomplishments a dozen more times, justifying my existence, attempting always to convince people that I mattered, that I *was* somebody.

In the evening after I came home from taking the GRE, I went to a church social event and mentioned to our new church's worship pastor that I could play piano in church sometime. I had studied piano as one of my two majors as an undergrad and had played for churches in college. Somehow here, though, I felt small again, a stranger in a new church, a person whose gifts, however earnestly I desired to share them for God's glory, still competed in a cutthroat competitive world. The longer the conversation lasted, the further I felt myself shrinking into my lawn chair. *So you majored in piano? How many years ago? Where have you performed? How much music theory do you know? Do you play only classical music? What churches did you play for?* I knew perfectly well this man's resumé: his years performing in Nashville, the summer he toured the country as keyboardist for a top Christian artist, the jazz trio he had started in his spare time, the blog he wrote with several thousand readers more than mine. He asked me to sit at a piano to play a couple worship songs, and there was nothing worshipful about what came off my fingers—just a lot of tentative plinks colored by self-depreciation and envy.

I respected his goal of not putting distractingly awkward musicians onto the stage in front of a congregation trying to focus on God, and the truth was I *didn't* have a lot of experience playing worship music, particularly songs that had come out over the past ten years while we lived overseas. His questions touched an already festering wound inside me.

The next time I sat down to play piano, all I could think was, *Is this good enough? Do I sound like an old grandma with a warbling voice trudging out "He walks with me and he talks with me" on an electric organ?*

Over the next months I played piano less and less. When I did, nothing inside me sang.

The same thing has happened at various times to my writing. Some days I sit down to write while a terrifying little voice inside me demands after every sentence, *Is this good enough?* Like most authors, I dream of pouring out streams of brilliance, but most days instead I wander into the kitchen to get another Oreo. I feel mostly like Anne Lamott's blunt description of writers who "do not go around beaming with quiet feelings of contentment. Most of them go around with haunted, abused, surprised looks in their faces, like lab dogs on whom very personal deodorant sprays have been tested."[6]

I know that writers, pianists and Ph.D. applicants are not the only ones who feel this way. Being cool must be about the most painfully unattainable ambition ever dreamt up. And yet we go on dreaming it up, generation after generation, as a load of bricks to carry around from puberty until death.

■　　■　　■

My middle school lunch room was situated in a long hallway, with a single line of plastic fold-out tables end to end all the way from the place they served our nachos and instant mashed potatoes on down to a back corner where the awkward kids sat—the ones in sweatpants, the ones with greasy hair, the ones eating free hot lunch every day, the ones who didn't know any new music. From that corner on up to the lunch ladies we middle schoolers silently and brilliantly organized ourselves into a hierarchy of cool. To sit at the cool end you had to plow people over in the mad dash to the front of the lunch line, or have friends who saved you seats, or have a loud voice or a boyfriend or better-than-average hairspray. Even then, many days you shoved your elbows out and jammed your butt cheeks down to make space. Meanwhile you performed great feats of conversational gymnastics to deny that you ever expended any effort to be cool. Being cool, like being humble or radical, is a perfectly elusive goal that you fail at the minute you reveal that you are trying to succeed.

I recall a certain brand of canvas shoes with tiny colored stripes on the sides that *everybody* on the cool end wore, or so I believed. The coolest kids had three or four pairs in different colors to trade with their cool friends. Gear like those shoes, I believed, got you to the cool kids' end of the lunchroom.

I would like to say that I was far too confident to play childish games of drooling over striped canvas shoes as the golden ticket to cool. I was not. I wanted them as much as anyone. I never owned them because I couldn't convince my parents to throw away the otherwise-good-but-not-cool shoes they had bought me before the school year began. Having a quiet voice and low tolerance for elbowing, I slid steadily downward, meekly claiming my seat in the medium-to-low cool zone. From there I still measured my worth by the same dumb standards, grabbing at any snatch of alternative proof of my value.

As we get older we find new variations on cool and new routes to the top tables. From striped tennis shoes we graduate into travel coffee mugs, Acuras, iPad 4s, Burley bike trailers and Ralph Lauren furniture. Those of us who steer clear of defining ourselves by our appearance and accessories seek out alternative names for cool—*successful, brilliant, world-changing, talented, anointed, influential, radical* . . . even *amazing*. We dream of collecting a few thousand friends on Facebook, or getting cast on *The Bachelor*, or breaking into the top fashion magazines with a signature line of African-animal-inspired children's headwear, or becoming an Olympic bi-athlete skiing and shooting our way to the top.

Even in some Christian circles, we find subtle ways to climb upward. We latch onto the latest and greatest terms in our theological radius: *emergent, radical, missional, neo-reformed.* We paddle harder to stay on the crest of the new trends. We set our sights on being the spiritual superhero, starting our own video series, visiting a hundred countries, drawing strangers in coffee shops into probing spiritual conversations, sitting on a couch beside a big-name worship leader, building a "movement." Or maybe writing a book about how many amazing things we've done in Nicaragua, China and South Africa. As Thomas Merton confessed even from inside his monastery walls, "Many of our own most cherished plans for the glory of God are only inordinate passion in disguise."[7]

■　■　■

Our years overseas gave us a side step out of the cool game. People around the world have their own various qualifications for cool and plenty of fears over whether their cell phones, clothes and shampoos (or lack thereof) are good enough. As outsiders, though, we didn't fit neatly into people's social categories, and so we often felt exempted from competition. Some days we were not just at the low end of the cool table but out the door and a block away.

In Nicaragua our village's baseball team asked me to serve as their *madrina*, a sort of half-godmother, half-mascot. Every other team's leading lady showed up in a ball gown worthy of a prom, but I never got the memo on the dress code. I marched in a parade between the beautiful princesses, then up to the center of the baseball diamond, in a big straw hat, an old plaid shirt and jeans rolled up to my knees. Still, our village seemed to like me anyway. They cheered as loudly as anyone when our team got announced. I was probably just weird enough to keep, kind of like an exotic pet—no other village had a white *gringa* for their *madrina*. I enjoyed living in places where most people didn't care if I didn't buy the "in" striped canvas shoes or missed the latest episode of the "in" television show, and where people actually said "You're looking fat" as a compliment.

Returning to the United States felt like the shock of arriving as the new kid mid–school year wearing the saggiest frayed pair of sweatpants, standing in the cafeteria searching for a place to sit. I could name only two current primetime television shows and even fewer popular musicians from the last decade. Still, we carried with us Adam's stunning photographs of overloaded African motorcycles and hut-dotted landscapes, stories of stomping on snakes and visiting dying people, plus my freshly published first book. These seemed to make up for the

One of many friends in South Africa who taught us to sing from the heart.

sweatpants. Plenty of people said we were amazing, that our life was worthwhile. They slid aside and ushered us into seats at the cool table. Or at least *a* cool table.

Even at the cool table, though, there's always the threat of getting beaten out of your little social safety zone. Whether I feel like I'm succeeding or failing, I still find ways to measure myself up in the cool competition. Like a hungry raccoon, I keep slinking back to dig into the same trashcan.

■　　■　　■

When my first book came out, nothing felt amazing. We had about 550 copies in boxes under our bed, plus the two on a bookshelf, the one in my computer bag, and the dozen or so in a box in my car trunk. I started writing blog posts on my new website, but no one commented. We left messages letting colleges and churches know I was available to speak, but they weren't clogging my phone line with requests. I read other authors' brilliant blogs with tens of thousands of followers and felt nauseous when I clicked back to see my own blog's little Facebook "like" counter ticking upward at the speed of dew forming.

When I read the newly released books that everyone who was anyone was reading or magazine interviews with big-name church leaders, I alternated between scribbling notes with jiggly excitement because I had struck on deep currents in the North American psyche and would sell a million copies of my books, and despairing that this proved I had already lost the race and was not original enough. Like finding another kid wearing the same sparkly shirt you got for your birthday, I kept coming face to face with proof that I was not original. We were writing for a "popular" audience not so different from the popular realm we judge ourselves within. Popular means we have to be original. We have to prove that what we are producing is like nothing ever created before, new and innovative and the next big thing. And at the same time, we have to prove it is just like many a successful hit that has come before, that it touches the trendy themes, that it is not, in fact, too original. This is the task of a writer.

It is also, I find, the tricky task most of us try to accomplish in life. We want to be fully original and also fit squarely within a narrowly defined "cool." We want to be adventuresome to the fringe and also comfortably safe. We want our children to be brilliant and also never to care whether they are brilliant. We want to look like we don't need anything and also never lack anything. We want to be able to apply for any job on the planet but not have to compete against seven billion other applicants. We want to reach our highest dreams, make something eternal, never have bad hair days and show off our bellies with meaningful but discreet tattoos and great abs.

Instead our bellies are slightly flabby at best. We are all still ordinary. We have limitations. We are not the magic key that unlocks the solution to the world's biggest problem, and nobody understands our three-hundred-dollar tattoo anyway. Most of our lives we've been told that we can go anywhere, be anyone and do anything. Supposedly whether female or male, tall or short, whatever our race or language or neighborhood, we can yank ourselves up by our paisley bootstraps, make something of ourselves, impact lives and leave a legacy. Instead we find ourselves in the medium-to-low end of the cool table. We become just another blogger without readers, just another cubicle jockey, just another short-term overseas volunteer who comes home and wonders if we changed anything. Since the economic downturn many of us have lost jobs, taken pay cuts, moved to smaller homes or collected consumer debt to our eyelids. We sit in our back corner tables and believe all would be well if we could just earn, beg, elbow or hairspray our way into a seat up just a little higher.

■   ■   ■

I talked about this with my friend Sarah, who got diagnosed with skin cancer when she was twenty-nine years old. She had basal cell carcinoma, the most common and treatable kind, not the really scary melanoma kind. Until she finally realized that the scaly spots on her eyebrow and back weren't going away, skin cancer was totally off her radar screen. To treat it, the doctors carved out the cancerous cells, layer by layer. In operating they had to gouge out half her eyebrow that would never grow back. The operations put her cancer into remission, but left her always on alert for more spots needing biopsies, always aware that her skin cells were plugging along toward cancer.

In the same year of her skin cancer diagnosis, her husband, Chris, lost his job. She agonized over whether to stay home with their two preschoolers or achieve a dream of becoming a graphic designer. Her gifts as an artist radiated in everything she touched, from her paintings on their walls to her precisely clipped haircuts. Why shouldn't she have a chance to share that beauty with the world, to have quality of life and let her husband search for a job he enjoyed, too. Instead too many things in their life refused to cooperate. They lived for a year with his parents while he substitute taught to make ends meet, then finally took a job in another city where they hovered in lonely confusion.

"When we got married I thought we'd have all kinds of beautiful adventures, world travels and successes," she told me. "Instead in a few short years we had a baby, my appendix burst, and then the skin cancer spots, and now a hidden-at-home life with kids and none of the professional and artistic success we dreamed of. I thought we'd do such amazing things, but what have we done at all?"

There was a pause in the conversation and I began mentally listing all that was amazing about Chris and Sarah. When Chris prayed before a meal, we always felt *prayed* for, not like it's some flowery antiquated words strung together, but like he's good friends with the all-powerful God. Sarah was gentle with her children, and she appreciated beauty more than almost anyone I knew. Every time we met she would tell me I was beautiful in some way, and I knew she meant it. I counted these qualities as amazing. But Chris and Sarah weren't often looking at themselves and seeing those qualities. The superficial gauges of coolness were all so hypnotic, so blinding to the real and valuable adventure they were living.

Later that day Sarah told me, "I feel like everyone's staring at this missing eyebrow." Beyond missing eyebrows, we both knew of plenty of holes in our lives that we imagined the world staring at, judging, condemning.

"So much of our lives we spend caring what we look like and worrying what other people think," she said. "But caring what I look like is such vanity."

What a great word. *Vanity.* She said it again. "Vanity—like it's all in vain. For nothing."

■   ■   ■

I heard a sermon about that word: vanity.[8] The pastor said that the word sometimes translated as vanity runs throughout the book of Ecclesiastes in the Bible. Solomon, who most likely wrote the book, spent a big flashy life earning fame as the wisest man ever to walk the earth, and then said this: "Then I looked on all the works that my hands had wrought, and on the labor that I had labored to do; and, behold, all was vanity" (Ecclesiastes 2:11 ASV). The pastor said that the word translated as vanity means a smoke, a vapor, a fleeting thing that wafts away into nothingness.

Then this pastor told us about Sandcastle Day. He described one morning each year when thousands of people descend upon a small-town Oregon beach to build some of the most elaborate sand sculptures in the world, masterpieces like entire veterinary clinic scenes and life-sized elephants emerging from the shore. And then, as the sun sets, the tide comes in. Wave by wave the ocean swallows the sandcastles back into oblivion. People stand watching the tide roll in, toppling all those beautiful human-made monuments.

That, the pastor said, is vanity. And that is what all our ambitions are: sandcastles in the tide.

I liked what he said, because I could relate to that feeling of wasting our lives on endeavors that would not matter at all in the long run: all my middle-school angst over hairspray not holding until the end of the day, and my recent distress over too few comments on my blog posts that would just keep sliding away into the past. Sure, all that was vanity.

As I thought about the story, though, I wanted to grapple with a little problem. The fact was, all those people were still showing up on the beach each year. Why did they come? Was it so wrong to want to participate in something fleeting? If, like the writer of Ecclesiastes said, all is vanity in this world and we're all just getting swept away like sandcastles in the tide, what are we supposed to do in the meantime? I pictured those people building their sandcastles. Some of them, I supposed, would come to win prizes and prove their skills. But most would be amateurs simply there to create. They came despite the hungry waves, or even, perhaps, for the very purpose of spiting them. Because participating in the joy of creativity doesn't have to be about seizing every day and putting it up on a bookshelf for everybody to admire forever. They came because spending a day with hands in wet sand arranging and carving out sculptures that have never come before and will never come again, even in the face of the end that comes to us all, is . . . fun.

I have watched my children play in that zone where time and tides don't matter. Zeke lines up dominoes for hours though they will work at most only once. Phoebe has started writing books about horses and whales, inventing a computer made of paper and a building replica of a Russian musical instrument only to throw these projects in the recycling bin when she moves on to another one. They write puppet shows and improvise songs heard only by the small audience of their two parents, never to be heard again. They are not out to prove to the world a long list of accomplishments. They build, play, interact and create because they enjoy it, because that's what life is for.

We're created in the image of a God who is a creator, and that makes us creators by nature. Whether being a creator means becoming something like a glass blower or a potter, or just means we initiate conversations, systems and interactions that shape the world around us into a better place, creating simply feels right. And creating well is the opposite of creating to get people to like you. It's about creating not to be loved, but because you're created in love, and love propels you to create more of that.

A carefree family sing-along around the piano

Whether or not Zeke's line of dominoes falls down perfectly, and whether or not Phoebe's paper computer keys move, we will always love them. One of my greatest hopes as a parent is that my children will soak up that love down to the tips of their toes and live in the freedom that comes from being loved.

■   ■   ■

I always figured when I came to the life stage of making choices about my children's toy purchases, I would keep my daughter out of the pink aisles of the department stores. No daughter of mine would determine her identity by the shape of a Barbie doll or the attitude of the Bratz girls. I wanted to save a future teenager from body image issues and gotta-be-cool middle-school angst. Keeping those impossibly slim hourglass-figure dolls with their glamorous wardrobes out of sight of little impressionable eyes seemed a good start.

Living overseas, our daughter's toy closet stayed mostly clear of unnaturally figured dolls for her first few years. Then, to my dismay, while we were on a return visit to my parents' home, little four-year-old Phoebe discovered a shelf full of the very Barbie dolls I had played with as a child. I watched her pull out one doll after another from the cupboard, and I forced myself to stay calm. I glued my eyes back onto the magazine I was reading, holding back the urge to snatch the dolls from her short little fingers.

In a few minutes, I heard her singing a little song she had made up. "You're beautiful," she sang, over and over. "Beautiful as the sun. Beautiful as the sun."

Not wanting to interrupt her moment absorbed in play, I peeked over my magazine to watch. Most of the dolls had fallen on the floor in a pile of crumpled ball gowns and tiny high-heeled shoes. Phoebe clutched just one doll in her hand. To my amazement, she was singing her song over a generic doll with wildly knotted dishwater-blond hair and a bald patch of glue on one side of its head. The doll wore a brown bulky dress my grandmother had crocheted out of leftover yarn, and my daughter was unsuccessfully trying to shove one fallen-off leg back onto its body. Compared to the other Barbies in their sparkling evening gowns, tiaras and pink two-piece swim-suits, this doll was a clear loser.

Here was a four-year-old girl, sporting her own stained sweater two sizes too big and uncombed hair sticking up sideways after a nap, knowing more about beauty than most girls four times her age. It was as if she already knew the meaning of inner beauty. True beauty does not depend on the details of outward appearance; it depends on the eye of the beholder.

I like to imagine that God holds me with the same unbiased adoration that my daughter sang over that ugly Barbie with, calling it beautiful. I imagine God calling me beautiful with the same words that can speak beauty itself into existence just as he created all things out of nothing.

It's not hard to imagine because, of course, that's exactly what God does.

God's standards for beauty, or success, or value, or whatever word we use for "cool," don't depend on the whims of fashion or corporate promotions. We each have a true beauty that is, as my daughter sang, "like the sun." The same Creator God who made the shining sun and stars also made us with an inner light to shine, and God makes no mistakes. No matter what the world says, God will always be singing over each of us again and again, "You're beautiful. Beautiful as the sun. Precious because you're mine."

■   ■   ■

Martin Luther figured that out when he was not four years old, but thirty-three. For years, as a well-behaved monk, Luther had been trying to figure out an answer to this question: "How can you become pious enough to please a Holy God?" I read that question in his biography when I was also at that third-of-a-life crisis age of thirty-three, and I saw there the same question everyone my age seemed to ask. We didn't use the word *pious*, but we filled in plenty of other similar words. How can you become successful enough? Influential enough? Popular enough? Good enough?

Then at age thirty-three Martin Luther got it: "All have sinned and fall short of the glory of God, and all are justified freely by his grace through the redemption that came by Christ Jesus" (Romans 3:23-24). There you have it, folks: we can't become pious enough. Or good enough. Or whatever enough. Trying to fill those holes is like dumping wheelbarrows of sand into the ocean to build a bridge. We just can't do it. We can't look good enough on the outside; we can't have everything all together in straight-enough lines to earn God's big stamp of approval. Even if we manage to earn the little stamps of other people's approval, they keep on washing off with the next rainfall.

There's no prize at the top of the cool charts. Instead the prize is already here, wherever we sit, as soon as we'll take it. The prize is that God loves us. Unconditionally. When we believe it, claim it and own it, we're free. God sent his son Jesus Christ to die for us generic Barbies with our legs falling off. That's called grace.

Luther put his revelation into words and tacked it up on the door of a church on a holiday when everyone was sure to be attending, and he blew their minds. That day pretty much started the Reformation—no small feat for a guy who was just a third of a century old.

Maybe by around thirty-three we're all ready for a little reformation wakeup call. Jesus died about that age, after all. It's a good time to ask what we're doing still living. It's a good time to ask if we've been trying to prove ourselves to a holy God who just wants us to stop trying so hard to impress somebody, who just wants us to let him love us.

Martin Luther uncovered this idea of God giving out free grace and love, but the grace and love wasn't something new. Just as Christopher Columbus didn't "discover" the Americas—they were there all along, and people knew them well and lived in them—Martin Luther didn't discover that people are not saved by works but by grace. It was there all along, and there were people living in it.

I'm glad he rediscovered it nonetheless. We all need to rediscover grace, maybe more than once in our lives. Maybe every day. There's a reason one of the most famous Christian songs ever written is called "Amazing Grace." Grace is amazing, and it frees us to live amazing lives. Without grace we're either living with elbows ready to knock people down on our way to the cool table, or we're losers sitting at the bottom of the table picking our noses because we believe the lie that says we don't matter.

I had narrowed life down to just two options: either play music for the tenuous approval of a fickle world, or play music not at all. I need to find the third way motivated by grace. I can loosen my grip on approval for a job well done but still hold tightly to all that is good and pure in that job. There is a fine dance in between, where I let every in-the-image-of-God gift that's been given me burst out in all directions. I can move undaunted by every other gifted soul in this world, thankful for their gifts too. In that fine dance comes the amazingness of grace.

That dance can lead a person to turn down a promotion up the corporate ladder to instead care for a relative with Alzheimer's. It can lead another to adopt a child with a severe disability, another to start an alternative microcredit program. It can lead, as it did for my friend Sarah's husband, to turning a deaf ear to the world's demands about using his college degree and instead taking a job he loves, baking artisan bread. It might lead, as it did for me, to pulling out a dog-eared book of music and singing my heart out.

There's something magnetic about people who are transformed by grace. They live completely certain that God finds them beautiful, cool, approved and beloved, so they never have to try to earn God's—or anyone else's—approval. They live not trying, but trusting. They live not accomplishing great things in order to be loved, but accomplishing great things because they are loved.

ORDINARY ADVENTURES
for the Uncool

- Cut your own hair.
- Invite over someone who's awkward.
- Dance in your living room at night with the lights on and the curtains open.
- Act in a community theater production.
- Try to surf.
- Wear your least favorite clothes to the mall and don't buy anything.
- Give compliments to everyone you see in a day.
- Sing on a city street.
- Skip.
- Have a day without talking.

6

ALL I GOT
FOR CHRISTMAS
WAS MALARIA

SUFFERING
Adam

Just after our first anniversary, we packed up an old suitcase and a hiking backpack and hopped a plane for Managua. We had made contact with a friend of a friend, a Nicaraguan who worked for a small Nicaraguan Christian economic development organization. This secondhand friend agreed to host us initially and to help us find a village where we could live.

She introduced us to a village named El Porvenir ("The Forth-coming"), and at the beginning of September 2000, we bumped up the mountain in the truck she had arranged for us. The forty families in the village had organized themselves as a cooperative to raise, harvest and sell shade-grown, delicious, organic coffee. Additionally each family had a small plot of land they maintained, where they grew corn and beans.

We slid out of the pickup and stretched. Looking at the courtyard, about a hundred children and a couple dozen smiling but reserved adults stared back. We plopped our twenty-year-old suitcase on a board that offered the only shelf in the small room in a barn that they graciously offered to us. A family down the dusty road offered us a *tijeras*. We weren't sure why they wanted to give us their "scissors," but they came back with a folding wooden frame with a plastic tarp nailed between it. This folded out into a super simple cot. It would be squished and sticky for two adults on tropical humid nights, but we would have somewhere to sleep.

And then I started to cry a lot. We were alone. Without an organization. Surrounded by abject poverty. Out in the sticks. Without electricity, vehicles, safe drinking water, health care or any way to communicate with a neighboring village (let alone our worried families). It seemed gutsy, brash and crazy. We knew it would involve some suffering.

I got more than I bargained for.

The first morning, we awoke sometime around 4:30 a.m. on our narrow plastic cot to the sounds of our new neighbors: doors opening elsewhere in the barn, coughing, noses blowing, the flip and flop of *chinelas* on feet walking past, the scraping of metal machetes on the sharpening stone, roosters crowing and low voices. I put on my leather work boots and stepped outside.

Our room was right in the middle of the village where the road widened out into a square of silty dust, with the barn on one side and the coffee processing shed on the other. Most of the afternoon, people would sit on benches and fences during the day, just watching life go by, but at

Adam catches some quiet moments at sunrise.

5:00 a.m. there was a buzz of activity, a tenor of expectation. It was a work day.

I was told to get my *pichinga* and *porra*, two words I'd not learned as a Spanish major at the University of Wisconsin. Thankfully, our neighbor Luz had prepared them: a water bottle and lunch pail. And our neighbor Luís lent me a machete that he'd sharpened for me to use. With that—and without any idea where we were going or for how long or what we'd be doing—I hiked down the mountain with the men of the village.

After about forty-five minutes of fast hiking down steep grades with big rocks and gnarled roots, we arrived at a fence line. We cut a few straight nine-foot-long branches and began a process of measuring off grids for planting fruit trees on the end of the cooperative's property. No problem—I had finished my one-and-a-half liters of water within an hour or so in the heat, but other than that, I was doing pretty well until we had to trek back up the mountain. My boots were concrete. My head, neck and torso were swimming in sweat. My lungs sizzled. My soaked shirt was flecked with grass bits and streaked with dusty paste. We worked for five hours and then had the fast, steep forty-five-minute hike. Luís was smiling and breathing normally when we got home. I walked a few more meters to our room and collapsed on the *tijeras*.

That was the first day.

■   ■   ■

Some weeks later we again hiked down the broken mountainside, this time to an open flat area of six-inch-tall grass. Some discussion ensued about the plan for the day. I couldn't follow it, and I wondered what we were going to do in a field of grass. The men started slotting in along one edge of the field. It was then that I realized everyone else had another implement that I lacked—an L-shaped stick that I later learned is a *gancho*. A quiet, young guy noticed my confusion and took me out to cut one in the forest.

I kept hearing the word *maíz*—corn—but didn't understand the connection. "Are we going to plant corn in this field?" My brow furrowed trying to unscramble the puzzle. Looking at where others had started trimming down the grass, I saw they were leaving some in rows. Upon closer examination, it dawned on me that there actually were already fledgling corn plants amongst all the grass. And our (my!) job for the day was to double over and ever so carefully (but quickly!) mow down all of the green, six-inch grass and none of the green, six-inch corn, with a machete and a hooked stick we had just cut off of a tree.

Life isn't all hardship in a forested Nicaraguan village: there's rarely a shortage of bananas.

Needless to say, a lot of my grass stayed up and a lot of my corn went down. And I was so, so slow. After ninety minutes, my back was starting to burn and spasm. I went to sit on a rock in the shade. I watched Don ("Mr.") Miguel—definitely older than my own dad—slice his way down the field and then start to walk over as I dried off my face.

He pushed his old baseball cap back on his head. "Este trabajo . . . es duro. Rinde a uno." *This work is hard. It's exhausting.*

No kidding.

I could have been back in the U.S. getting a master's degree or Ph.D., or working a white-collar job and pulling in a decent salary, driving a nice car and moving up the ladder. Instead I was holding a machete, sweating like a glass of sweet tea in summertime and trying to not swear or cut off my toes.

And then Miguel went back into another row, chopping his way away from me. I managed to hack my way through a few more rows and haul my sorry self back up to our windowless barn room to lay down and wonder, *Why in the world have you brought us here, God?* More tears.

■   ■   ■

I often asked the same question when we first returned to the United States eleven years later, after our years in Nicaragua, China and finally South Africa. I saw no clear spots for me, a writer/photographer/teacher with experience in poverty alleviation projects. I seemed an outlier in any application process, often under qualified, sometimes over. This was the season in which I spent hours pacing back and forth on the burnt orange shag rug in the double wide trailer where we were staying. I was trying to think, worry and walk my way to a solution, to answer all the questions we packed in our suitcases when we returned to the United States. I contacted the local university with some of my shots of their baseball team's recent game, trying to drum up a freelance gig. I wrote to well-connected people I met at conferences to see if they knew of anyone who might need a guy with my skills. I searched online for publications that both seemed like they might want some of my work and seemed like they might pay. The life of a job hunter or freelancer sometimes feels like selling vacuums door-to-door. "Look, it really works! It will make your life easier! Please—oh please—buy this vacuum!"

In the midst of this circus of self-promotion and looking for work, I thought back on those hard days of work and trying to figure out what I was good for in Nicaragua. After several weeks in El Porvenir, we figured out one reason the work was so hard for me.

■   ■   ■

My symptoms built up over a couple of months. First I was generally run-down. I attributed this to the heat and the hard work, maybe exacerbated by the lack of vitamins and minerals. Then I noticed that my abdomen was kind of bloated, like the carcass of an animal that's been in the hot sun for a few days. Next I started burping. That's not normally a big deal. But when your burps come frequently and taste like rotten eggs (and you've not had an egg in weeks because a plague killed the village's chickens), you know something is wrong. I guess having diarrhea for a few weeks also clued me in that I had a problem.

We thumbed through our copy of *Dónde No Hay Doctor* (*Where There Is No Doctor*), deciding that I either had giardia (from the water) or brucellosis (from the raw milk we had a few times).

So one day, we hopped a ride on the 1972 Ford 5000 tractor to the nearest city, León. We found a clinic, waited, saw a doctor, got referred to a bigger clinic and waited some more. Then a nurse said she needed a stool sample and handed me an empty Gerber baby food jar.

Sure enough, giardia lamblia had set up camp in my guts. I got some meds to take over the next two weeks to kick it in the teeth. A week after I finished the treatment, I was burping sulfurous nastiness again. About that time, I got a letter from a friend who had been in Bangladesh and had giardia so bad that he was sporadically incontinent. Upon returning home to the U.S., doctors were close to quarantining him because nothing could get the beasties out of his belly. Hearing that, I decided I would just live with them, my tummy buddies, for the rest of our year there. After all, they were endemic in something we were eating or drinking, so it would just come back, I reasoned. And then upon returning to the U.S., I could be quarantined and that would make a good story for a book that I would write years later about suffering.

And thus the stage was set for my year of bloating, stinky egg burps, lethargy and weakness. It was usually tolerable, but one night I was up for the fifth time, sitting in the latrine that I came to know very well, killing spiders and watching for scorpions. Liquids poured out of me, leaving me weak and chilled in the moist, warm night. Then a new sensation swept over me. I swung the door of the latrine open in the moonlight, and in the midst of yet another diarrheic surge, I threw up in the moonlight.

When liquids come out both ends at the same time, it's pretty bad.

Around this time, we had three separate people quote to us James 1:2-4:

Consider it pure joy, my brothers and sisters, whenever you face trials of many kinds, because you know that the testing of your faith produces perseverance. Let perseverance finish its work so that you may be mature and complete, not lacking anything.

When I was sitting in a latrine half the night and throwing up out the door of the thing, the last thing I wanted to be told is to consider it "pure joy."

And that's how it is whenever I'm facing anything difficult—I don't like it, I want it to end, I fight it, I whine, I complain.

■   ■   ■

Shortly after the doctor diagnosed my giardia, Christmas came, and we were excited to host Chrissy's family for a visit. The day before we were to head down to the city, I got sick—really sick, not just giardia sick. Really sick.

I got weak by mid-morning. I laid down and that didn't really help. Then I lost my appetite, a rarity for me. And then the fever hit.

My temperature climbed: 100. 101. 102. 103. 104. We watched the mercury thermometer we brought keep ascending. I started to lose my ability to concentrate as the evening loomed. The sun set on Chrissy trying to read in *Dónde No Hay Doctor* by flashlight to discern what might be happening, how serious it was and what she could do to make sure I didn't die on top of a Nicaraguan mountain.

Her research pointed toward Dengue fever or malaria. In any case, she needed to treat the symptoms. I felt frigid, but my fever stayed up in a dangerous range. She followed the handbook's instructions, stripping off my clothes despite my feeble, delirious protest and swabbing me with a damp cloth to cool my overheated twenty-three-year-old body. This was torturous. I was lying on our cot, shivering in a pair of shorts, with Chrissy making me still "colder." My teeth were chattering as my body burned. I was afraid the noise would keep our neighbors in the barn awake.

Eventually I got to sleep, and the fever broke as the predawn nighttime sky began to gray. At 5:00 a.m., Chrissy got me dressed and into the wagon of the trailer, sitting on the spare tire. We bounced down the mountain behind the big blue Ford tractor.

Six hours later, we got to Managua, got some medicine and received Chrissy's family. Joy to the world, indeed.

So between work, giardia, malaria and a general sense that our work wasn't helping our friends in El Porvenir much at all, my attitude and sense of identity were at all-time lows. Why were we there? Why was the God I followed not caring well for me? Would our time there help at all? Why wasn't I feeling blessed when I was with the poor who Jesus said were blessed?

■   ■   ■

One evening in February, I was lying in bed at the house of a relative of the old banana-and *mamei*-stealing woman named Yaya. I had just broken my ankle while hiking there. Yes, broken. Well, there was no x-ray to be had, but it felt the same as when I broke it in China three years later. Yes, my ankle. Yes, while I had giardia and generally felt worthless. I sunk deeper in the mire.

We had been talking about how long to stay in Nicaragua. Originally we had planned to stay until we reached the one-year mark from the August when we arrived. Lately I had been begging for us to leave sooner. Surely another month would be enough, or maybe just another week, or how about we leave tomorrow?

Laying on their plastic cot, I cried. Again. Why? Why! Why . . .

And then, with my leg elevated and throbbing, with *zancudos* (mosquitoes) buzzing about, in a baking hot-tin-roofed home, God spoke: "You're staying until August."

I winced. I knew these words flashing to mind were not self-generated, even by my subconscious. A few times in my life, I'd experienced this sort of nearly audible, surprising and indisputable guidance from Jesus. It makes me uncomfortable. But like those other touchstone moments, I knew this was bigger than me.

I cried more.

A few weeks later, with resolve hardened by that moment, I booked our return tickets for August—the first day of August. I was obeying, but just barely, as that was all I could bear.

■   ■   ■

Sometime soon after my ankle healed, we were over at Juana's house. Juana was sassy, loud and an *evangélica*, a Protestant Christian, one of very few in the village. Since we didn't have a cooking space in the barn where we lived, we had an arrangement with El Porvenir: we would be adopted by a different family every month. They would feed us and teach us things, and we would help out however we could in their household economy.

For Chrissy, this meant making tortillas, carrying water in buckets on her head, washing clothes with the women, teaching a few adult literacy classes a week, and keeping families company through the long hours of cooking and cleaning and some home garden work.

For me, this meant heading out to do the backbreaking labor that made me cry.

But one night, we did something different. We were together at Juana's house, with her husband, Tomás, and their four kids.

Juana finally finished her work and sat down on an overturned five-gallon bucket. "Dime un cuento, Adán y Cristina." *Tell me a story.* So I looked at Chrissy with a smirk. "What story should we tell?" Chrissy had been telling fairy tales to kids and sometimes their moms for a while, but this was my first chance. Juana gave us the opportunity to share something familiar and to laugh. I launched into "The Three Billy Goats Gruff." Her little girl couldn't stop giggling each time I used a high scratchy voice for a goat. The firelight from a rag wick stuck in a glass bottle of diesel fuel illuminated expressions of delight on the faces of everyone, from Juana down to her little five-year-old son, Juancito.

As we walked home in the moonlight, on the dusty road up to the barn, I turned to Chrissy. "Well, even if nothing else, we sure do provide a lot of laughs for them."

And that night, between nights of tears and sore muscles and loneliness . . . that night, that was enough.

I try to remember that stories matter. The Israelites were supposed to remember and retell them, Jesus used them, and we're supposed to keep living them. The big story focuses on a cross, an implement of torture and death. Jesus, the Creator as a creature, said I have to take up my cross every day. I don't want to run from risk, escape suffering or enfold myself in anxiety. But I usually do. I don't want to organize my life around seeking comfort and security as much as I do, but we North Americans sure like to. I don't like it, but I think I've seen Jesus the most clearly and concretely right when I'm the most desperate and trembling. At other times his action and the reason for our risk and pain can be hidden, even for years.

■   ■   ■

El Porvenir was a coffee-producing cooperative. The year we were there, the world coffee market went into a tailspin, dropping to the lowest prices in fifty years.

The village couldn't sell their coffee, even just to break even. They would do better not to even harvest it, letting tons of certified organic coffee beans rot in the forest.

As a coffee lover (and someone who cared about our friends there), I thought I could help in this one area. I started going down to the city weekly, making calls, visiting people, trying to find anyone who was dealing fair-trade coffee from Nicaragua. As a twenty-three-year-old I had no clue what I was doing. "What are the laws and tariffs on Nicaraguan exports? How do you buy a shipping container? What's the best way to contact Starbucks?" I eventually found a cooperative in Managua that was looking for certified organic beans from small producers and would pay fair-trade prices— about double the market rate at the time. That would make it worth the trouble of harvesting and even put a solid profit in the pockets at El Porvenir.

Through word of mouth, I heard of a man named Marcos, a gringo who was part of a coffee-buying co-op. I asked our village's coffee-producing co-op leader, Raúl, to head down the mountain with me to meet him. They had actually heard of one another but hadn't met, and my neighbor was skittish at first. I explained that I thought it was probably a good idea, as they were actual buyers and wanted to pay a fair price for organic beans. All went well, and after a few months, a hundred phone calls and a thousand questions, a deal was done. I had connected Raúl and the coffee cooperative to good people, and it was at just the right time. They got a great price, and this all made sure our friends—all forty families—would have a pretty good year. Even with giardia in my guts, I felt pretty good that day. But within a week, I was thinking more about my sulfurous burps, the latrine and my inadequacies than anything else. It's hard to gain perspective, and it's very hard to keep it.

Ten years later, Chrissy and I were speaking at Calvin College's Faith and International Development Conference in Grand Rapids, Michigan. They had a fair-trade fair. We were trying to buy some gifts for friends we were going to visit. I wandered over to a table and picked up a bag of coffee.

Raúl's picture was on the bag.

Chills ran up my back. With tears welling up in my eyes, I stuttered to the bewildered student selling the coffee, "How do you have a picture of my friend on your coffee? I know him. I've eaten in his house. Chrissy! Come over here! They have El Porvenir coffee! *Chrissy!*" And I ran away from the table with the bag of coffee in hand, unpaid for. I would gladly endure giardia for another year to have that feeling again.

It turns out that for ten years, my seemingly serendipitous connection between El Porvenir and the co-op in Managua had been bearing fruit. They kept this reliable buyer at a great certified-organic and fair-trade price. Moreover, the buyers brought volunteer teams to provide basic health care, from vaccinations to dental care. They helped put in a well at the bottom of the mountain and ran water pipes all the way up the mountain to the village. They built a small school so they no longer had to meet on the patio of the barn where we'd lived.

My stupid, painful, diarrheic year actually did a whole slug of good for people in El Porvenir. It sure doesn't happen all the time, but sometimes God does amazing things through our grumpy obedience in the midst of suffering. And once in a while, we even get to see it.

ORDINARY ADVENTURES
in Perseverance

- Fast.
- Measure how much water you use in a day and try to carry that much water (or even a fraction of it) from the nearest natural body of water.
- Live for a week without using electric lights.
- Eat a simple meal resembling that of a Majority World country.
- Attend a church service that's in another language.
- Count how many things you've quit in your life and ask why.
- Meet refugees in your city.
- Spend thirty minutes considering how your life could be worse.
- Walk somewhere far (like to Walmart, Tennessee or Belize).
- Talk to someone living on the street.

7

WASHING MACHINE GUILT

MONEY
Chrissy

Now and then old college friends still refer to Adam as the guy who ate food off of returned cafeteria trays. In college he used to walk into a dormitory cafeteria, stroll into the room where people slid their finished trays into tall carts and peek from one tray to another looking for food. An untouched muffin here, a half bowl of fries there, and his meals were made. A lot of days he'd hardly have to purchase any food. I cannot tell you how many people were grossed out by this, and I was one of them.

And yet he made his point. It was the ultimate "You better eat that up because children are starving somewhere" object lesson. I guarantee everyone who sat at a table with him while he ate a stranger's leftover carrot cake thought twice the next time they got a dessert and didn't finish it.

I stuck to the societal norm that eating from a stranger's plate has something inherently dirty about it, but like Adam I was itching to find ways to challenge people about how to use resources. I had taken a course called Malnutrition and World Hunger as well as a couple classes in the African Studies Department, and I was all too aware that people were suffering in Africa and little places we'd only just heard existed like Moldova and Tonga. I had read Thoreau's "Civil Disobedience" for an English class and was quite taken by this guy who stopped paying taxes and went to jail to stand up against the injustices he saw in slavery and war. Meanwhile Adam took a class about Gandhi, the epitome of civil disobedience, who made salt, spun his own clothes and lived as a locavore long before the term existed. Plus we were reading the Bible most days, which is hard to do for long without stumbling across passages like, "It is easier for a camel to go through the eye of a needle than for someone who is rich to enter the kingdom of God" (Matthew 19:24), and, "Whoever oppresses the poor shows contempt for their Maker, but whoever is kind to the needy honors God" (Proverbs 14:31). We studied all these guys who wholeheartedly put their money—and their time, safety, careers and reputation—where their mouth was. We were ready to figure out what we believed about money and justice and then live that out whether it clashed with our neighbors or not—and perhaps all the more so if it clashed.

So we became known as the dating couple who were ridiculously extreme about the use of finances. We fasted at a ministry-hosted banquet in protest of what we thought was a misuse of funds. We were voted "Most Likely to Give Away Their Last Dollar." We led a book club on Ron Sider's *Rich Christians in an Age of Hunger*. We sponsored children overseas. Adam offended a friend by questioning why he spent his money on hair gel.

At our wedding, I wore a homemade dress, and after the ceremony we changed into jeans and big T-shirts a friend gave us that said "I got married and it was cool." We served spaghetti and a big sheet cake with whipped cream and strawberries, and, instead of spending on decorations, we just let people hike around enjoying the wildflowers and cliffs of a camp where we had worked. We asked for no wedding gifts, but our generous friends and family wrote us checks anyway, so we saved them up for our first international plane tickets.

We lived our first year together in a little apartment with a bedroom so small we put our mattress on the floor without a bed frame and walked across it to reach the other side of the room. We inherited plastic blue-green dishes from my grandparents and found furniture on curbs and in coffee shop basements. Paychecks from a mishmash of part-time jobs added up in a savings account for a year. As he finished his degree, Adam worked one day a week in a bakery. I taught piano, played piano, served in a restaurant, substitute taught and filled in as a halfway house manager. Our freezer and refrigerator were always packed with day-old bread from the bakery where Adam worked, day-old muffins from the restaurant where I worked, and bruised fruit and expired yogurt from the food co-op where I volunteered, plus venison from the deer Adam and his dad hunted.

Every week when Adam came home from the bakery he brought huge garbage bags full of day-old five-dollar artisan loaves of bread that the bakery would otherwise throw in their dumpster, and we would play "Bread Fairy," driving around in our little maroon Plymouth Horizon hatchback, dropping bread loaves at friends' houses and dorm rooms. We held a lot of parties, packing people into our little apartment and opening our doors across the hallway to neighbors who invited their own friends. Those were cheap and joyful days, rich with community, simplicity and the conviction that we were going somewhere. Joy mattered, and having fancy stuff didn't.

■   ■   ■

Then came that year in Nicaragua, the second-poorest country in the Western Hemisphere. Clinging to Jesus' statement that "blessed are you who are poor, for yours is the kingdom of God" (Luke 6:20), we went looking for God's kingdom among the poor. We lived in abject poverty with no power, no safe drinking water, no transport, no cell phones, no health insurance and no hospitals within five hours. Over the whole year, we spent only $4,000, which included gifts for every family that fed us, bus rides into town every couple weeks, a "vacation" to a coastal island on the other side of the country, round-trip plane tickets from Wisconsin, a small library for the village and Bibles for every family.

No matter how much we tried to live like our neighbors in Nicaragua, we found ourselves terribly, awkwardly rich. We might have worn flip-flops like theirs and learned to swing machetes and shape tortillas alongside them, but everybody knew that we had bank accounts, college educations, and networks of friends and family back at home. We sat down to meals each day through the driest months of the year beside families who had not a single coin in their homes and had stopped buying even sugar, oil and rice. Some days the only food they had was the corn and beans they grew, and they were fortunate not to have run out of those from the last harvest (yet). People sat in our tiny room touching and adoring everything that didn't come from Nicaragua—tubes of toothpaste in brands they had never seen, our tennis shoes, our Nalgene water bottle. Before we came to the village, Nicaraguans in the city had told us to buy a two-inch-thick foam mattress to place on the three-foot-wide cot we slept on. After a few months in the village we realized we were the only people with a foam mattress. Everyone else slept on the plain plastic cots stretched between boards, or hammocks. Some kids slept on boards. Kids came and sat on our cot and squished their hands into the thin foam and marveled, "Qué rico." *How luxurious. How rich.*

About once a week I would go to the big concrete reservoir that collected rainwater and stand alongside a group of women, each with a flat rock in front of us perched on a frame of logs lashed together. We would place one clothing item at a time on our rock, splash on water from a bucket, rub the clothing with a bar of laundry soap and scrub them clean. One day a woman asked me, "Cristina, is it true that in your country you have machines to wash clothes?"

I searched for some non-self-incriminating response, feeling the pressure of all the women awaiting my answer. But what could I say? "Oh, of course there are such machines, but I don't use them much," or "Well, yes there are washing machines, but now that you've taught me how you live here I'll go back and never use a washing machine again"?

I said a simple "Sí," and wished I could crawl under my rock.

To my surprise, there was no reproach in the women's response. "¡Oh, qué rico!" they marveled. "If we had washing machines, how happy we would be! Oh Cristina, when you go back to your country, you have to enjoy those washing machines."

They didn't want me to feel guilty. They wanted me to enjoy washing machines, foam mattresses, cars, ovens, communication conveniences and whatever else life had somehow given me instead of them, because they sure would if they had them. Before coming to Nicaragua we had read enough news and statistics about poverty to expect that people here would be pretty miserable. There was no doubt these people lived in poverty, but what surprised us was that most of the time, people weren't miserable. In fact they generally seemed as happy as any North Americans I had known, and some I'm sure were happier. Sometimes they shocked us at how "irresponsibly" they spent the few coins they had on frivolities like little bags of chips for their kids. Who were we, though, to say they shouldn't take the money they earned only a couple times a year for selling beans or coffee and spend some of it for pure fun? We watched the smiling faces of the kids sharing their potato chips with buddies, and we joined the occasional parties where people feasted on their only iced drinks and meat in six months and danced into the night. Most of these people weren't wallowing in misery for lack of money, and they didn't ask us to be miserable either.

Still, living in Nicaraguan poverty left deep impressions not easily forgotten when we walked into malls and grocery stores in the United States. I would stand in beautifully decorated homes back in Wisconsin remembering that my friends in Nicaragua asked us for leftover newspaper pages to paste on their walls as wallpaper. I would walk into grocery-store aisles with fifteen brands of diet instant frozen meals and remember that my friends in Nicaragua could slice one golf-ball-sized onion to season eight meals of rice and beans. Maybe my friends in Nicaragua didn't want me to feel guilty about the opportunities and wealth I had, but I couldn't figure out how else to feel.

■   ■   ■

When we lived in China, even with a newborn, we still lived simply by some standards. Phoebe slept in a portable bassinet the size of a car seat for nearly a year and everything we took to China still fit in three suitcases (up from two suitcases to Nicaragua). Already, though, in China we were living several rungs up the economic ladder from Nicaragua. We had a furnished apartment with some heat in the winter, a DVD player and a computer with Internet access. A bowl of noodles outside our apartment cost the equivalent of twenty-five cents and even at the nicest restaurants in our neighborhood meals cost less than three dollars. We ate out for nearly every lunch and dinner and felt rich.

When we started looking for jobs in Africa, we ruled out jobs in countries where English wasn't spoken and with landmines, coup threats or constant temperatures in the triple digits. We moved to South Africa where our Zulu friends taught us how to use the first cell phone we had ever owned. Our neighbors of European descent taught us to eat the thickest slabs of grilled steak we had ever seen and to wash them down with the robust local red wine. In South Africa we lived in constant tension: richer than many neighbors who had no electricity or car, but not so rich as many people we knew.

We learned when we arrived back in the United States that we were not rich by United States government standards either. Having lived at something like a middle-class South African standard for the last few years, our income fit snugly beneath the federal poverty line for Americans. We qualified for free health insurance, food stamps (the Supplemental Nutrition Assistance Program) and free school lunches.

I mentioned to Phoebe that some kids don't like to talk about getting free lunch because they are embarrassed that their families are poor.

"But we're not poor!" Phoebe scrunched up her forehead and laughed, shaking her head as if us being poor were as ridiculous as finding an ostrich in our bathroom. She had seen slums in Nairobi, mud-brick homes in South Africa and people begging on the streets of several countries. She knew plenty of people who happily hopped in the back of our car because they didn't have cars. She could remember the six months in Africa we hadn't owned a car but felt rich in friendships because other people gave us rides. Whenever we had needed school books or housing or electricity, we could

Some South African friends pull out their toys—a collection of bottle caps—and the kids play happily for hours.

supply those needs. Though we rarely bought extravagant foods, we cooked foods we loved and treated our bodies to healthier foods than many people could afford. Our children knew that in South Africa they had more toys than any-one in our apartment building, and as far as I could tell, our children never considered themselves poor. And yet here in America, somebody had decided they qualified as poor. This did not compute.

■   ■   ■

We lived in the tension of middle-class angst. We knew we had so much more than many people in the world and our lives could be much more difficult, but we were also constantly reminded that we had so much less than many people and our lives could be much easier than they were.

Sure, we weren't poor compared to most people in the world, but the fact was, those free lunches were a big help to our budget. While I was speaking at a gathering of college students during our first months back in the United States, I happened to mention during the question-and-answer time that we had qualified for government health insurance, Medicaid. A young woman asked accusingly, "And you took it?"

I wanted to say, "No, I left the health care money for people who needed it more, because of course we're fine." Instead I stammered an evasive response. The truth was, Medicaid meant we saved thousands of dollars over the first few months back in the United States, and we were thankful for a government that could help when people no different from ourselves didn't have jobs that provided insurance. When Phoebe came down with a cold that dragged on into four-and-a-half weeks of coughing, I couldn't have been more thankful that I could show up at the doctor and get her treated without losing sleep over the cost. When we learned we got free school lunches and food stamps, we celebrated. We went and bought olive oil, healthy yogurt without mystery ingredients, dried apricots and a bag of frozen fish fillets. That night Zeke prayed over the dinner table, "Thank you God that the government gave us this nice food."

Still, as healthy, Midwestern, middle-class white people, we faced plenty of pressure to not admit we take government support. Settling in the United States meant figuring out how to budget money under constant pressure to be independent, to not ask for help and to make yourself look presentable. I quickly tired of being the one who dragged her kids to a dozen garage sales every Saturday, whose kids rode hand-me-down bicycles that always had flat tires or falling-off chains, who made her own bread and granola even though her kids wanted white squishy bread and Golden Grahams, who kept making those foods not just because they're healthy and special and fill one's house with the aura of simplicity and warmth, but because they're cheap. I still used a pair of glasses I bought for eight bucks in China seven years earlier. The one time in the year that I stepped up from Goodwill and bought a clothing item in a mall just before a speaking engagement, I deliberated for half a day before making the unfortunate choice of an overpriced fifty-dollar shirt that ended up making me look more like an elf than a public speaker. For haircuts I went to a place where stylists in training cut hair for next to nothing. Sometimes I came out a rock star. Other times I came out Ramona Quimby, age eight. I was tired of being That Thrifty Lady.

In the United States it was not easy to sustain that memory of ourselves as "not poor." We started with the cheapest-package-deal life we could find and quickly felt pressure to move up. After six months in the doublewide trailer, we rented an apartment in Madison, Wisconsin. We filled our apartment in a frantic rush, taking whatever free stuff people offered, happy just to have something besides lawn chairs to sit on in our living room. A year later we were ready to sell the wet-dog-smelling riveted pleather recliner that we got for free, and we replaced our grungy $50 couch with a couple cleaner ones on Craigslist for $150 each.

We were really moving up in this world.

With every step up came pressure to move up faster. We looked around at peers coming home from cruise vacations to new Pottery Barn furniture in their five-bedroom homes. They were nice people, and who were we to judge their lives?

Even when I tried to go simple, life didn't feel simple. I saved money by making canned applesauce and ordering huge sacks of flour and oats from some nice Amish people my friend knew. Then when I cooked all the applesauce and got all the flour sacks home, I had to go out and buy more canning jars and more plastic tubs to store the sacks in. I wanted to learn how Amish people store their half-empty flour sacks without buying lots of plastic tubs.

At another gathering of college students, an eager young man stood up and asked, "How are you going to live differently in the United States now, having seen what you've seen overseas?"

I wanted to answer, "I have no flippin' idea. That life is a million miles away."

■   ■   ■

Already our monthly budget was three times what it was in Africa. Living simply and intentionally felt impossible. Adam turned a corner and bought himself hair gel, the very stuff he'd criticized somebody for years earlier. I felt like middle-class America said I needed multiple mobile devices, high-speed Internet, gymnastics lessons, water park trips, a car for me and another for Adam, insurance for our cars and our home and floods and fires and for our very lives. And I was supposed to have a big house in a nice safe family neighborhood with an excellent school, diverse enough to say it's "quite diverse" but not diverse enough to the point that we become a minority.

The apartment we moved into in Madison was bright and clean with tall ceilings and big windows. But it was small—very small, we learned, for a family of four in middle-class America. The night before we moved in I stayed awake imagining how we could possibly fit our stuff into the two closets in our bedroom. Then when I got there, I saw I'd remembered wrong: there was just one closet. I let out a little noise like I'd been hit with a basketball in the head.

The kids shared a bunk bed in one bedroom; the other bedroom doubled as our bedroom and my office. The other large room was a combination kitchen and living room. The bathroom was the only room not doubling as anything. We argued over whether to put the kids' beanbag in the back corner or the front corner of their bedroom.

There were no other choices to make—nothing else could budge.

I like to think we could have lived happily squeezed into that two-bedroom apartment for years just because people around the world live with so much less space, but honestly it got old fast. We had to shush the kids every time they laughed hard and constantly tell them to stop jumping (which, if you've ever watched a five-year-old, you know they do frequently). Our downstairs neighbors regularly took naps in the afternoon and complained liberally to us and the management. We couldn't do laundry after eight at night. We couldn't use the sustain pedal on my electric keyboard because they could hear it clicking from below even if I used headphones to keep the whole keyboard silent. We couldn't invite over families with more than one very quiet child. If Jesus hadn't said so explicitly "love your neighbor," we would have given up trying.

Home-ownership was not a next life stage we wanted to jump into lightly though. We knew there were hidden costs and plenty more purchases to deliberate that came alongside the obvious mortgage payments. We had heard friends tell how with a house, you can always fit another painting on the wall, another toy for the kids, an upgraded television. Then you need the furniture to match, the time-saving gadgets to give us more time to see the kids and the TV service to make the television worth the price. Meanwhile the property taxes and utilities cost about the same as the rent on a four-bedroom apartment. We knew people who had virtually disappeared from social circles as they spent every evening and Saturday fixing up wood floors, stripping wallpaper and carpeting basements. We knew plenty of people struggling to stay financially afloat. When these same people graduated from college and got their first "real-world" job, these engineers, teachers and physical therapists felt like they earned a fortune. Compared to the pittances they had lived on in college apartments eating frozen pizzas, they felt like kings. A few years later they were looking around at everything they "should" be buying and feeling like paupers. Even without a house, we were starting to relate.

Buying a house would be the ultimate step for us in settling down. After living in eighteen homes in our twelve years of marriage and moving between those homes at least twenty-five times, settling down in our very own home and putting down roots sounded awesomely, terribly momentous.

■   ■   ■

There's a pattern in the Bible that people who settled down and got comfortable don't tend to fare so well in their relationships with God. In Revelation when Jesus gave different messages to seven different churches, it wasn't the church that was suffering afflictions, poverty and persecution that got in trouble. Jesus told them, "I know your afflictions and your poverty—yet you are rich!" (Revelation 2:9). Instead it was the church with plenty that got in trouble. Jesus told them, "You say, 'I am rich; I have acquired wealth and do not need a thing.' But you do not realize that you are wretched, pitiful, poor, blind and naked" (Revelation 3:17).

In the Old Testament, the Israelites settled down into their Promised Land after years of seeing God's miracles as they escaped slavery and hiked across the desert. It was there in the settled land that they kept returning to more and more corrupt practices and forgetting about God (Judges 2:19). Just as Moses warned them before they got to the Promised Land,

> When you build fine houses and settle down, and when your herds and flocks grow large and your silver and gold increase and all you have is multiplied, then your heart will become proud and you will forget the LORD your God. . . . You may say to yourself, 'My power and the strength of my hands have produced this wealth for me.' But remember the LORD your God, for it is he who gives you the ability to produce wealth. (Deuteronomy 8:12-14, 17-18)

While a part of me was more than ready to settle down, I already felt the weighty mental and spiritual responsibility. In many ways, I would have been happy if Jesus would have just asked me, like he did the rich young ruler, to sell all my possessions and give them to the poor (Matthew 19:16-30). I would have gladly been one of the people in the early church who shared everything in common, selling their stuff and giving the money to anyone in need (Acts 2:42-47). Jesus might be asking some of his followers to go off and live on the street or in other people's spare bedrooms or in communes, but it seemed pretty clear that Jesus wasn't asking that of us specifically right now. Instead we had to figure out how to put food on the table and put couches, coffee tables and wall hangings in our own living room, and still follow him. I definitely felt like I was trying to squeeze my camel hips through the eye of a needle.

I knew, though, that plenty of other people, even in the early church, had dealt with this same dilemma. One of my favorite Bible passages for wrestling through this question of what to do with money comes from Paul, advising Timothy about what to tell rich people:

> But godliness with contentment is great gain. For we brought nothing into the world, and we can take nothing out of it. But if we have food and clothing, we will be content with that. . . . Command those who are rich in this present world not to be arrogant nor to put their hope in wealth, which is so uncertain, but to put their hope in God, who richly provides us with everything for our enjoyment. Command them to do good, to be rich in good deeds, and to be generous and willing to share. In this way they will lay up treasure for themselves as a firm foundation for the coming age, so that they may take hold of the life that is truly life. (1 Timothy 6:6-8, 17-19)

I love how much joy is tucked into those verses. God provides us with stuff for our enjoyment. Those Nicaraguan women wanted me to enjoy my washing machine, and so did God. Jesus went to parties thrown by rich tax collectors and went to weddings where he supplied the wine. The prudes of his day called him a drunkard and a glutton because he refused to live by legalistic rules of what you could enjoy and with whom. I wouldn't prove anything to God by trudging or boasting through life with as little stuff as possible. If I was measuring myself just by keeping up with the Joneses or by proving my frugality to the radicals, I was going to miss out on a Christ-centered life. We might have a kitchen table with six different chairs, unframed wall hangings, and a 1995 Ford Escort with rust-rimmed wheel wells and over 200,000 miles, but these didn't make us holier people, especially if we were going to whine about them or be proud of them instead of being content with them.

■   ■   ■

A big piece of recentering our financial perspective has always come through practicing generosity. We had long since realized that generosity doesn't always just come spontaneously spilling out of us, so we set up monthly direct deposits to our church and ministries we knew were doing good work. Each month we start by giving a solid 10 percent of what we earn no matter what purchases we have to make or what the rest of our savings account looks like, and then when spontaneous urges and appeals come up we try to respond above and beyond that baseline.

Giving away money is joyful and freeing, but I don't think it's an excuse to do whatever we feel like with that remaining 90 or whatever percent left for ourselves. Even if only 75 percent remained, or even 25 percent, we would still be soaring above the billion people in the world living on less than two dollars a day. Just having over $2,200 of *assets* (not income) each puts us in the top half of adults on the planet, wealth-wise. We had more worth than that much just packed into the six suitcases we carried back from South Africa, let alone in bank accounts and storage closets back in the United States.

Sometimes I wish that Jesus were just a little more legalistic and would give us a nice spreadsheet of where every percentage of our money should go each month. It's not easy living in conversation with God over how we use our resources. It means sometimes God says, "Sit tight and be content with what you have." Other times God says, "Look at what needs someone else has and help them out." Other times God says, "Don't waste your money on that junky purchase because it won't make you happier anyway. You're better off sticking that money in a savings account for a time when I have something better to do with it."

For years God had taught me about finances as we raised money in order to do our work overseas. This process of "raising support" (common amongst Christian "parachurch" nonprofits) forces us to look hard at what we're doing with our lives and check whether it's worth the money people give us to do that work. It also forces us to acknowledge that money is God's to begin with, and it exists to get God's work done, one way or another. At the end of the day, that's true for us whether we get money from gracious friends and family for our work with a ministry, or if we get paychecks from more traditional jobs. There's no shame in earning money, whether a lot or a little, to accomplish God's work. It's not as if we get to hold the only key to a locked vault with our money inside—eventually (or today) God might have better use for it somewhere else. Managing money well doesn't mean we never spend money. Sometimes we spend like crazy. The trick is to spend it where God wants it spent. Sometimes it's hard to be content with what we have. Sometimes it's even harder, though, to do nearly the opposite, to spend lavishly. Either one can get in the way of us taking hold of "the life that is truly life."

■   ■   ■

For the first half a year that we lived in our apartment, we checked real estate listings regularly and often spent Sunday afternoons at open houses. One day we spotted one particular house on a two-

and-a-half-acre plot just a half-mile from the city limits, surrounded by state and county parks, with forest and fields and a 130-year-old farmhouse perched on a hilltop. As I recall, God said nearly out loud, "Would you just look at *that!*"

We did.

This was a place that we knew we would not only be richly blessed by ourselves, but would have unique opportunities to bless others. We calculated the children's bedroom to be more than twice as big as their current room, and we would have a guest bedroom besides. We imagined an addition with a big dining room for parties and a wood stove to heat the home using trees from our forest. We stomped through the snow around the house to pace out garden space. We checked out library books on sheep, chicken coops and tree houses. My mind leapt to prayers for a family to buy a farm next door or help start a community-supported farm or perhaps a bed and breakfast or a restaurant employing inmates returning from prison or inviting in refugees or raising alpacas and miniature ponies, or . . . Yes, God, we could see the possibilities in that.

At the current list price, the house was not in our budget. We made our first offer $80,000 below the list price. We sent that offer just before Christmas, imagining ourselves homeowners by Valentine's Day.

How wrong we were. The seller was moving the lot lines on the property, which needed town, city and county approval, each granted at meetings a month apart with delays every time. We entered the longest string of negotiations and waiting our real estate agent had ever experienced. The price crept slowly down as we sent back counteroffer after counteroffer, negotiating a well-sharing agreement, driveway installation and dozens of other considerations we never knew were possible in buying a house. The price slowly inched down toward what we could afford without getting ourselves into financial trouble if our kids needed braces, the water softener blew up or the rusty 1995 Ford Escort needed replacing. As weeks dragged into months, with every price shift we kept asking ourselves, what is this place really worth? What makes it worthwhile at all?

I remembered the feeling eight years earlier when we were planning to go to China and needed to start raising support for the first time in our lives. We sat down with the paperwork for the organization we would work with and added up what we needed to live on. The cost was not small. It was not an investment we made logically based on financial returns. This was money spent down the holes of mailing costs, airplane flights, meals and health insurance. We knew, though, that China was where we needed to be. We trusted God had work for us to do there and people we needed to meet there. So we counted up the cost, gave up higher paying jobs we could have found somewhere else and raised that money. Now we were counting the cost again and getting ready to splash some serious cash.

God was asking us to trust him. He knew very well what we needed to live, whether it was going to be in this house or not. Some days in those months of trying to be content with our little apartment, I wanted to say, "That's real sweet of you to tell me I can wait, God, but mind your own business because I have already decided that I *do* need this right now. And I can tell that I need it because I really, really *want* it."

■   ■   ■

During those months, Phoebe had made up her mind that she wanted to buy an MP3 player. She had saved up money from Christmas gifts and lemonade stands and coins picked up off parking lots to somehow acquire upwards of seventy dollars. We were trying to teach our children the same lessons about money we struggled to learn ourselves—to consider purchases carefully, to be generous first, to share, to be content. Our general suggestion to our kids when they wanted to spend more than a couple dollars of their money was that they "sleep on it," or as they often said, "sleep over it." Phoebe had been sleeping over this MP3 player purchase for a while, and so, when she spotted one for twenty dollars at an office supply store, she was ready to dish out her hard-earned cash.

All went well until Zeke, standing in front of all the pretty machines, suddenly burst into tears. "I want to get this one!" He flailed and snatched up the nearest package in front of him, a $129 music player. When I told him to calm down, stressing that he could share Phoebe's new purchase, he turned to me in all-out weeping. "I want to spend my money! I want to buy something! But I don't know what to buy!" I calmed him down slightly as we walked toward the registers, only to have him latch on to a monster-shaped pen and key-chain at the checkout counter for the hefty price of three dollars. In a hurry, Adam smartly refused to consider it. Zeke wept his way out the door.

Ah, the curse of it all. Money burns holes in our pockets and we crave the thrill of spending it even on overpriced stuff we never wanted anyway.

That same day, Phoebe lost a tooth. At night she tucked the tooth into an envelope under her pillow. Zeke also had a plan. On a slip of paper, he spelled out in five-year-old spelling a note to the tooth fairy: "I want to by a pen." I believe it was his way of secretly asking permission of someone other than his parents, permission to spend frivolously but not feel disappointed afterward.

The tooth fairy wrote a note back to Zeke: "Thank you for your note. Maybe you should think about the pen for a week and then decide if it's really what you want."

It was the best I could come up with at 10:00 p.m. Sometimes I wish the tooth fairy would just teach my children how to spend their money wisely and generously, conscious of both generosity and savings. I wish she'd tell them once and it would be done for life. And while she's at it, she could teach money management to the rest of us too.

Zeke didn't get his pen, and we didn't get our house yet either, but as the months passed we found plenty to enjoy in life without either of them. One day we made a list of our favorite things about living right where we were living. Phoebe listed catching butterflies outside by the big rock across the street that she had named "queen rock." Zeke listed the neighbor's dogs and his first school only a block away. I listed the neighbors on our block who we had gotten to know; the library, the grocery store and the zoo all close enough that the kids and I could bike there; and the way our family hung out together in the one big living room space. Adam listed the world's biggest Bratwurst Festival that happened in our neighborhood, the independent coffee shop overlooking a lake two blocks away, the ice-skating rink down the street, and the snow fort he and the kids built in an empty lot across the street. Looking at the list, we realized suddenly again that we were very, very rich, no matter what other people might think.

■   ■   ■

"You have the smallest house in the whole world," Phoebe's second-grader friend said when she came to our apartment for a play date. Phoebe looked on the verge of tears as she put on her hat and scarf to walk her classmate home with me.

"Oh, I've seen smaller homes," I said as we climbed down the stairs. "I've seen . . ." I let the words fade out. It didn't seem like this kid was about to be changed by a list of people in the world living in far worse conditions.

The girl had been begging me for more cashews for the last half hour. Zeke had gotten the cashews as a Christmas present and he had generously offered to share. We usually ate about four cashews in a sitting because they were so precious to him.

"I go crazy for nuts," she said as she chewed. Zeke stared at her as if checking for signs of craziness breaking out as an al-

"I go crazy for nuts."

lergic reaction, watching his precious nuts disappear. She kept grabbing them by the handfuls until I discreetly closed the cover.

"What's *that?*" the girl had asked when she spotted Phoebe's new doll, a Christmas present Phoebe had looked forward to showing to doll-loving friends. Originally Phoebe had wanted an American Girl doll like many of her friends had, but when I explained that they cost over $100, she maturely and carefully chose a soft, cuddly and flexible one from T.J.Maxx that she liked better.

Now her friend eyed up Phoebe's doll. "What is she, some kind of baby edition?"

"Just a nice doll. She's her own thing," I jumped in at Phoebe's defense.

Her own thing. I was proud of my daughter for trying to be just that, but I knew it was not easy for her. Phoebe set aside the doll and suggested they play Candy Land. The friend lost. The play date had gone poorly for both girls.

A month earlier, before a play date with another friend, Phoebe had broken down crying at bedtime. "I'm not even looking forward to her coming. She's going to say my room is boring and small."

I mentally replayed what I had seen when Phoebe had played at this friend's house—a full-sized jungle gym in her basement, elegant hardwood floors, piles of dolls. Phoebe has just this one doll, tucked in a bed she made of paper, beside the bunk bed she shared with her brother.

"Phoebe," I had said, trying to reassure her, "you guys will find lots of fun things to do. We can go skating . . . we can make a list of fun games . . ." She grew quiet and I wiped her wet cheek, kissed her and turned out the light.

I had slept poorly that night.

We lived near the university, which most people said was a good thing because with all those professors' kids, the school earns high ranks. It was also unfortunately the second-least racially diverse school in the city and probably one of the least economically diverse too. And those professors' kids sure had nice houses.

Now Phoebe trudged along behind her cashew-loving friend as we walked her home. Phoebe blurted out, "I don't like dolls." Her friend looked at her own feet as she hurried ahead, kicking through the snow. "Well I don't like games."

Sometimes I forget how blunt kids are. I imagined the girl's report to her family when she got home: "They have the smallest home in the world. They won't let me eat cashews. They play dumb games." We arrived, and she ran into her house without saying goodbye.

When Phoebe and I turned around for the walk home, the sky felt bigger, bluer. "Phoebe," I said as she came up next to me, still wearing a near-tears expression. "Do you think it was annoying when she kept saying our house was so small?"

"Yes." Phoebe looked up at me, probably surprised I said aloud the potentially naughty thoughts she'd been thinking.

"Me too." We walked a bit in silence. "I guess a lot of kids think life is about having lots of stuff. Lots of adults think so too." I thought for a minute about what to say next. "But we know it's about more than that, don't we?"

She said nothing, but kept up beside me, and I could sense her stress dissipating. This was not an easy lesson. Both of us probably would be learning and relearning it for the rest of our lives.

Suddenly her face brightened as we passed under a shop's awning and she looked up. "Hey, can you lift me up to touch that icicle?"

"Sure." I grabbed her waist and lifted. When her hand touched the icicle I squealed, sure it would fall on us. The awning swayed and we both giggled and hugged as I lowered her to the ground.

In that moment a man on a bicycle swerved past us on the sidewalk. I noticed the grin spreading across his face as he watched us.

He must think we have a pretty great life, I thought.

And we did. Even without that house.

ORDINARY ADVENTURES
with (and Without) Money

- Save receipts for a month and total up where your money goes.
- If you're in debt, get someone to help you make a plan to get out and stick to it.
- Invite a friend to join you in a day of extravagance.
- Find a friend to share a lawn mower, rake, shovel, chainsaw, car, bike, washing machine, Crock Pot, fancy set of dishes, snowblower, printer, drill, television, tent, motorcycle, folding table, ice chest, waffle maker . . .
- Sponsor a child.
- Sleep over your purchases.
- Hang up your laundry instead of using a dryer.
- Buy dry goods in bulk at a low-price store.
- Learn how and why to cook simply (for ideas see *The More-with-Less Cookbook*).

8

THE
HONEYMOON
NEVER ENDS

MARRIAGE
Adam

In the year we moved back to the United States, we celebrated our thirty-third birthdays, and we also celebrated eleven years of marriage. We had lived a third of a century, and we had lived a third of those years together. This gave us some reason to pause and ask, "How is this whole marriage thing working out?"

Through most of the years in college, including the year we began dating, Chrissy envisioned herself graduating and immediately busting out of the United States to live in a hut in Middle of Nowhere Africa. Near the end of her junior year in college, after we had been dating for a year, she started filling out an application to serve with the Peace Corps somewhere in Africa. Then I caught wind of it.

"Um . . . what if we got married instead?"

What I said probably wasn't quite that pointed, nor did we consider ourselves "officially" engaged. But I realized I really didn't want Chrissy to head off for a two-year commitment, leaving me alone for my senior year and then clueless about what to do my first year out of school. Because of my Spanish major, I pitched a case for her holding off, hanging around with me to finish my last year and then going off to do good somewhere in Latin America. I still don't know what God did in Chrissy's heart in that conversation, but she put away the Peace Corps application and never got it out again. Instead we got married. I sure hoped she and I and the world would be a better place for having made that trade.

■   ■   ■

We don't think everybody needs to get married in order to go overseas, or to serve well, or to be happy. Quite the opposite—goodness knows we have plenty of single friends who are living better adventures than us, not sitting around pining for somebody to marry.

Our friend Betsy, another North American trying to do some good in the world, ran the microfinance project in South Africa before we did. She went on to support several dozen South African women who cared for several hundred orphans and sick people in an area where 40 percent of adults were HIV positive. We met Betsy when she was single and debating whether she should go back to the United States. She had reached a point in life where she really wished she were married, and she feared growing old wondering if living in South Africa was keeping her from finding a husband in the U.S. She decided to stay in South Africa. She continues to do great work there. And while life doesn't always go this way, Betsy ended up marrying a wonderful South African man and they now have an adopted son. I know those two are especially glad she stayed, but so are all the many people she has served. And I believe Jesus is too. It should come as no surprise that a woman who had been so committed to serving God single would serve God just as well married. And we know other people who were happily living Amazing Days without a wife or husband at their side.

I entered tentatively into marriage. There are advantages to being single. After all, Jesus and Paul looked at singleness as a privilege, a special calling to not be distracted by spouse and kids. I know very well that a lot of my time goes toward loving Chrissy (and Phoebe and Zeke). That is time and energy—love—that could be given to others. Could God really want us married if that might mean less good service to people in hard places? With questions still percolating at least a bit in the background, we tied the knot.

I quickly found that marriage is no magic cure-all.

■ ■ ■

I cried almost every day of our first year of marriage.

I was a twenty-one-year-old senior at the University of Wisconsin. I didn't really know anybody within ten years of me who was married. I moved from a plugged-in campus community to an apartment with my *wife*. I was unmoored and probably kind of a weirdo to my friends. They didn't know what to do with me (not to mention my wife), and I couldn't articulate what I was missing from them. I knew I needed to grow up, to take responsibility, to earn some money, to care well for my wife and grow with her, and to prepare for life after my impending graduation. I suddenly felt a lot of pressure. I went for long walks alone. I worked early mornings in a bakery. And I cried.

That's not to say that starting off our marriage was all bad. In fact, we had heaps of good fun in that first year. For our honeymoon, we headed down to the state of Georgia to live for a summer with an organization that was helping refugees get settled in the United States. Along the way we took a week without any plans and camped and explored from the Midwest down through the Great Smoky Mountains and into northern Georgia. We stumbled upon the WA-Floy Retreat Center in Who-knows-where-ville, Tennessee, and stayed for a couple nights watching peacocks strut around the trees outside our cabin window. We hiked a section of the Appalachian Trail. We went skinny-dipping behind our campsite in some Kentucky state park. We made bean and cheese burritos on our little camp stove in the gravel parking lot of a cool little Baptist church on a quiet country road, laughing at our funny, blessed new life together.

I was torn about not doing a honeymoon the way people expected us to ("You're going to serve refugees for a honeymoon?") and still wondering if we were actually better off married to live out what Jesus taught.

Partly to assuage my guilt for not jetting off to Cabo for a typical honeymoon, partly to keep some honest joy and celebration as we went about serving, and partly just to push the future and the magnitude of our commitment out of my mind, I started saying, "The honeymoon never ends!" I made up my mind that we were going to make sure we kept having a great time, finding romantic moments and places, exploring this great big fun world *together*. At a minimum, it meant putting a romantic spin on Amazing Days. And maybe it would even move us to live out more Amazing Days, to exercise more faith and to have a marriage that mattered.

Initially, this shift into "married mode" was hard and didn't seem like it was giving us more Amazing Days. But "the honeymoon never ends" was a step for us toward more Amazing Days and more adventurous and better living. It was a proclamation of joyous hope that our being married would make us more capable and effective than we were while single. I doubted it sometimes, but this silly phrase gave me a scimitar to slash at the doubts.

■   ■   ■

So the times when Chrissy was whacking a dishwasher or crying in the afternoons over a speech she had to write weren't the first occasions we had worked through one of us doing a lot of crying. Whether it was me slouched on a picnic table trying to figure out how to relate to my friends as a married guy, or me massaging my injured ankle on a Nicaraguan hillside, or either of us doubting whether we could live a meaningful life as plain old North Americans, that same commitment to live an endless honeymoon has dragged us through good times and bad.

In getting married, we were making a commitment to love each other intensely and joyously, and it's a commitment we've practiced seriously. Rather than a few pictures from a short expensive honeymoon cruise, we collected a mountain of images of what our life together meant over eleven years together:

- When we had fifteen neighbors over to our tiny college apartment for my "Dessert for Dinner" birthday party, Chrissy was there as the hostess and chief cake baker. (It became an annual tradition.)

- When I was giggling as we skipped across the waves in a motorboat off the Nicaraguan Caribbean coast, hoping not to throw up my coconut and mango diet, Chrissy was there.

- When I carried a heavy backpack of Bibles, treats for our host families, mail from the U.S. and a rat trap up the mountain to El Porvenir, Chrissy was there. (And her backpack was probably heavier.)

- When I broke my ankle playing basketball in China, Chrissy was there, taking me to get a sketchy x-ray and a sketchier cast and crutches that were six inches too short, and subbing to teach all my classes for two weeks.

- When in China we visited the hometowns of our students, who had never heard the name of Jesus, Chrissy was there.

- When I found out I was going to be a father, Chrissy was there. (Duh.)

- When our truck broke down in a South African desert, Chrissy was there (reading the Chronicles of Narnia out loud to our kids in the twelve inches of shade beside our truck).

- When I was pickpocketed and ran down the thief, Chrissy was there.

- When I felt like dropping Zeke off at the Humane Society, Chrissy was there.

- When I grieved a friend's divorce and prayed for another's leukemia, Chrissy was there.

- When we reveled in a cool sunny day in a canoe on a lake in northern Wisconsin, Chrissy was there.

Broken down along a South African desert roadside, Chrissy snaps a picture before settling into the shade beside the truck.

Through it all, Chrissy's been at my side, and that's a big deal. Our Amazing Days overseas grew into amazing years. Sometimes staying at each other's sides is the easiest, most joyful place to walk. If we're honest, though, there are also plenty of photographs we'd rather not take, of times when we might have wished I'd sent Chrissy off to the Peace Corps.

■   ■   ■

Soon after I said "I do," I realized all kinds of things I didn't like much about Chrissy. Sometimes she thinks I'm juvenile. She says "um" too often, has a mole on her back, spells poorly when she's working fast and insists that any bag with a zipper be fully zipped before it's ready to go in the car. And Chrissy would be just as quick to point out that I've gone through some awful hairstyles (picture Ronald McDonald), I check to make sure we have our passports several hundred times before traveling, and I fart.

These things really don't matter, but for any newlywed man (or woman), it's stuff like this that gives a serious case of buyer's remorse. "What have I done? I have to live with this? Argh!"

But the truth of the matter is that I'm just as weird and sinful, and the evil in this conflict is that I am selfish. (And so is Chrissy.)

Being married actually kicked my selfishness up a notch. Marriage has shown me my sin, my failings, my weaknesses, my pettiness, my pitiful selfishness. We went from carefree lovebirds to overlords of warring fiefdoms, feuding over toothpaste brands, the frequency of fast food meals, who makes the bed and when, who drives, what movie we'd rent, and whether we'd get a schnauzer. And it quickly escalated to how much we'd sit and talk, relationships with extended family, investments, sex, kids, birth control, career paths, which church we'd join, and where to live.

All this unearthed my deep-seated preferences, needs, desires and attitudes, and a surprising number of them ran counter to Chrissy's. It hurt a lot to recognize and try to release my own selfishness. Accountability is inherent in marriage. For the first time since I was a little kid, someone was seeing me from the time I woke up until I slept again, seeing the me that's me when nobody else is around. Whatever act I kept up for other people was too tiring to hold together 24/7. That's what life as a Christian is about—"[Jesus] must become greater; I must become less," we read in John 3:30. That means I embrace the purifying fire of sometimes not getting the kind of cereal I want.

Or the country I want to live in.

■   ■   ■

Around Christmas in 2001, we were at a Moravian church in the United States where Chrissy played piano and organ. I listened to the choir sing and looked up at a multifaceted, three-dimensional star hung for the Christmas season, representing the star that led people to Jesus. As I looked at the intricate paper craft that went into this large twenty-point star, I was overcome with an incongruent impression: "You're going to China." Clear as a bell, it registered like "You're staying until August" a year earlier while I was lying on that cot in Nicaragua with a busted ankle. That sort of thing doesn't happen a lot for me, so I take it seriously (and remember it).

Since coming back from Nicaragua five months prior, we had been wondering what was next. We were live-in caregivers for an old gentleman, and we both taught at a technical college. I was also a medical interpreter, and Chrissy taught and performed piano too. All these odd jobs were not our long-term plan. Our time in Nicaragua had raised a lot of questions for us, and we hoped additional training would make us more useful in appropriately addressing the challenges of global poverty. We were considering graduate studies in a field that would help us serve along those lines. I'd even gone far enough to investigate some programs, deciding that Eastern University's M.B.A. in international economic development would be the program I wanted to do if we did pursue degrees.

China had also been on my mind a lot, as I suppose it had for a lot of North Americans. China was changing fast, as were the ways the West related to China. The 2008 Olympics had just been awarded to Beijing. China entered the World Trade Organization. Some friends of ours said they had seen firsthand how the country was opening up and new ideas were being considered, including more and more people following Jesus. I started to get eager to find a way to live in China during these exciting times.

When I raised the idea of us serving in China, Chrissy's reaction ranged from skeptical to closed. She had wanted to live in Africa since before she knew me, and she put that off to get married. I was a Spanish major, so I was mostly responsible for talking her into going to Nicaragua. Now, just when we were ready to get some training that would help us do something good for people somewhere in Africa, I wanted to run off to China. To Chrissy, this was unreasonable, nonsensical and out of the question.

Then Chrissy saw a magazine ad. It was for a Christian organization that placed English teachers in China. And they provided additional master's-level training for a few degrees from a few institutions, tuition-free. One of the institutions was Eastern University. And the degree they offered in the program was the M.B.A. in international economic development that I wanted to get.

Chrissy held the magazine in her hands for a long time considering whether to show it to me or hide it in the bottom of the recycling bin.

She showed me, and I, of course, took it as something of a sign that we could both be in China and get the exact degree I wanted *for free.* Chrissy voiced concerns, still thinking she'd hate China, that she wanted to be somewhere in Africa. She harbored a suspicion—a hope—that something would happen that would keep us from going to China. Little did she know, there was something happening that might have kept us from China, but that story will have to wait for the next chapter. Meanwhile her complaints were softly voiced, as she wanted to be sure she heard right, that she didn't unnecessarily squelch my vision from the Moravian Christmas service. As our departure grew near, Chrissy's concerns were all bottled up, and the pressure got intense.

Six weeks before we were supposed to leave for China, we were at a Bible study group in the home of some friends from church. At the end, when we moved from looking at the Bible to prayer requests of the people who were there, I shared how people could pray for us in our final preparations to leave. Then Chrissy started talking. And crying.

"I don't want to go to China!" Sob, sob, sob.

I awkwardly looked around, wondering if people would still pray for our final preparations to leave.

They didn't, of course. We all first turned to Chrissy. They asked questions, handed her tissues, held her hand and helped us sort out what on earth to do with the calling I thought I'd heard for us.

A couple days later, I met with our pastor at the time, Rick, to talk about the situation. I was only twenty-four years old and had a lot of questions about how to make decisions in marriage, about passages that seem antiquated about women being submissive to their husbands and men loving their wives as Christ loves the church. He explained how these passages from the Bible played out in his marriage. One time, when he and his wife, Anne, had a big decision to make, it became apparent they were leaning in opposite directions from each other. He made space for her, saying, "If you think this is dead wrong, we're not going to do it."

That wasn't what I expected him to say. I had heard preachers say how Christian men are supposed to lead and be strong. And I also had heard others explain how those passages were culturally bound and draconian. Pastor Rick was saying, if she's unable to go along with it, don't charge ahead, *even if you are pretty sure the Lord Almighty spoke about it.* He said something like, "The Bible says 'Husbands, love your wives as Christ loved the church.' It doesn't say, 'Drag your wives around wherever you, Stubborn Brute, think she should go.'"

Pastor Rick shared how when Anne felt safe to really analyze, feel and contradict, she had space to properly consider the issue. And Rick got to really hear and consider her perspective. Of the three times they'd hit a serious impasse, Rick and Anne had ended up going with Anne's leaning twice and Rick's once. And that one time, he said, "I've heard you, and I think I understand. But I still think we need to do the other thing." Anne felt heard and loved enough to trust Rick at that point.

So I went home and said, "Chrissy, if you think you can't go to China or that it's wrong for us to go to China or that you can't walk with me on this one, we're not going."

She looks back now and says that was exactly what she needed to hear.

When we were just arriving in China six weeks later, we heard Peter, a Christian from Australia who'd been there a long time, make another point that was just what we needed to hear. He told us what he considered to be the most important thing for a married couple to remember as they serve overseas: "You're on the same team." It's a very simple distillation of marriage vows, of the commitment made on our wedding day. Simply articulating the five words, "We're on the same team," gives us perspective, whether we're facing a hard choice, annoying each other or butting heads (and trying to fight fairly). The obvious corollary is that it's a good idea to marry someone that you want to be on a team with for a season that often lasts fifty years.

Stealing a kiss in a restaurant in Thailand

I wish we'd had this advice *before* arriving in China. We could've used it. But it works just as well in the United States.

■   ■   ■

I *need* Chrissy. What I would have meant twelve years ago is much different than what I mean when I say it now. The first time I saw Chrissy, I was hooked, even though I had a different girlfriend at the time. She enraptured me. (Okay, she was very fond of baggy overalls and sweatshirts when we met. Chrissy's not the kind of woman who cares much about how she looks. She only owns about three outfits and doesn't really do makeup.) But I was caught in her snare, so much so that I dreamed about her months later (still having only spoken with her for a few minutes). And that dream led to us getting married.

But now, back in the United States, I can look back on our years overseas and see that my need for Chrissy has been not only romantic, but practical. If I was not with Chrissy, I would probably be totally screwed up. Of course I suspect God would have worked on me in other ways. But as it is, I see that God used Chrissy for a lot of good work in my life. Without Chrissy, I'd . . .

- watch standup comedy for hours

- eat pork rinds

- watch the games of professional sports teams that I don't care about

- never dust or clean my bathroom

- run around the world every few months or years in a desperate attempt to break into war/disaster/crisis photojournalism

- own a $3000 road bicycle, but never ride it

- get into weeklong funks of self-doubt, self-loathing and self-destruction

And not only would I be going off the rails in all kinds of ways, I'd also have missed out on all kinds of good stuff. Being married to Chrissy helps me step toward what is true, excellent, beautiful and worthwhile. She has pushed me to be a better writer. Heck, she pushes me to be a better *man*. Just having someone so close, I find my shortcomings are put in stark relief. I take better care of my body because I know someone's going to see me naked. Knowing that someone else knows when I get up in the morning and when I turn off the lights at night keeps me from working too hard or watching too many movies. Chrissy keeps our financial books, and that helps me give money away. Living with such a good cook makes me more comfortable inviting people over for dinner. She's pressed me to serve well and long overseas, even when it's been hard. Together, we've untangled languages and people and cultures. I've not done everything as well as I'd like in the past twelve years, but without Chrissy, I certainly would have done even worse. I probably would've snapped, given up and headed for a screwed-up life of odd jobs and too much takeout food.

I asked Chrissy what she'd be like without me and she said, "I'd probably be a lonely freakish woman living in an African hut, owning only about *two* outfits and never combing my hair and trying to carry out some grand obscure research but mostly beating myself up for not getting more done. And I wouldn't be a mom. And I wouldn't be writing this book, or any books, because you're in my books, and you're my biggest fan."

I think that means she doesn't regret trading her Peace Corps application for a marriage license.

■ ■ ■

Living in abject poverty in Nicaragua, in a Communist bloc apartment in China and in a thatch-roofed house in South Africa, I was extremely grateful to have Chrissy at my side. Through sickness and health, through want and wealth, through thick and thin, through joy and sorrow, through success and rotten failure, Chrissy was there. Like we promised from the start, she will remain here for me, and I for her. I especially love that she remains with me when one of us gets a crazy idea.

A basic rule of improv acting is to say yes to anything proposed. We try to live the same way. This mode of living has had us move to Nicaragua, make muffins for grumpy neighbors and start a Ph.D. When Chrissy or I voice one of these "what if" ideas, we smile and say, "Amazing Day!" thereby prepping ourselves to live out whatever craziness we have just uttered.

I'm sad that sometimes it seems our churches often lack such faithful imagination, an adventurous expectation of Amazing Days,

of "What is the Spirit doing next?" Christians are often just as
content with the status quo as the rest of society. Jesus and his disciples said really hard stuff that we don't seem to consider seriously:

- "Sell your possessions and give to the poor" (Matthew 19:21).

- "Those of you who do not give up everything you have cannot be
  my disciples" (Luke 14:33).

- "When you give a banquet, invite the poor, the crippled, the lame,
  the blind, and you will be blessed" (Luke 14:13-14).

- You "will do even greater things than these" (John 14:12).

- "Look after orphans and widows" (James 1:27).

- "Worship in the Spirit and in truth" (John 4:24).

The church is the community with which we live these out, and
our marriage is also to be a picture of that. As Jesus loves the church,
I'm to love Chrissy, even to the point of death. And she's to follow
my lead.

Further, though, our relationships to the church in North
America ought to be a bit more like marriage. We're not made to
glibly hop from one church to another. In each of our overseas
homes, we found a church. Each one had its issues and things we
would change. Sometimes we were bored. Or procedures didn't work
well for our kids when they were little. Or people got on our nerves.

Welcome to church, folks.

We need a small band of people to whom we commit and who
commit to us—to share burdens and to encourage each other to live
out the great news of Jesus. We have felt this need intensely while
overseas. And now, in returning to the U.S., we know it's essential.
Here, the dominant consumerist culture is so pervasive, so strong,
so effective at selling, that we do not have a hope of not being sucked
in, victims of very convincing marketing. Our companies are now so
good at it that they get our friends to market their stuff to us on their
behalf. Without a group of people carefully considering what is true

and how we ought to live, we are gonna get run over by a bus covered in logos and driven by Mark Zuckerberg. (And I don't say this lightly. Facebook is part of my job at InterVarsity.)

I need church. We all do—singles, marrieds, kids, divorcées, widows, whatever. We're not complete without it.

■   ■   ■

We all need a team. Marriage, at its best, provides a deep level of support and accountability that's hard to find in our isolationist culture, even within our churches. Whatever our team, we have work to do that's outlined in the ancient Scriptures. They read like a recipe for some Amazing Days, far beyond heli-skiing or hitching across Central Asia. Living those out in the United States means figuring out how to interact with people and live intentionally in different ways than we would in Africa or China, but it's equally challenging anywhere.

In the best moments in our marriage, we've provided each other daily accountability to live out the extremely hard calls to faithful living. Having a partner with me who has been a part of all the past thirteen years of adventures reminds me of what we hope the next thirteen will look like. As I look ahead, I'm thankful that I've married someone who can look at the Scriptures, bust my chops and say, "Why don't we live this out?"

ORDINARY ADVENTURES
with the One You Love

- Hold hands in public.
- List your faults together.
- Pray together.
- Throw a "Dessert for Dinner" party.
- Play basketball together.
- Move to China.
- Go back to a favorite place from early in your relationship.
- Say you're sorry (again and again).
- Spend an evening together looking at photos.
- Spend a week away together.
- Cry together.

9

Baby
Slaves

PARENTING
Chrissy

I used to think life ended with parenting. Not end like I'd die, just end like the me who had purpose, direction, career, style, romance, humor and friends would dissolve into an unrecognizable smear in the parking lot of Babies "R" Us. Or two burglar characters from a movie I never chose to watch would tie me up in the newly painted pink and yellow nursery bedroom closet. These intruders, "Mommy and Daddy," would hold my life hostage.

As if through the slats of the closet, I would hear Mommy telling my friends about stroller brands, bowel movements, childbirth and Winnie the Pooh. Mommy would go to mommy groups. She would worry about diaper rash and teething and school districts and choking hazards and at what age a child learns to walk. She would stop caring about people around the world except when pictures of goopy-eyed African kids suddenly shot pangs in her heart as she imagined her own children having goopy eyes, and she would send off a twenty-five-dollar check. She would shop for little plastic cups of chopped peaches and Sponge Bob "fruit" gummy snacks and call it enough of an outing for a day. Mommy definitely, assuredly, would not be amazing.

Meanwhile Daddy would go off, tired, to his eight-to-five job, stopping on the way home to buy diapers, frozen dinners and butt-rash cream. He would come in to find Mommy crying in her baggy sweatsuit, whining that she expected him home sooner. He would find a bucket of board books overturned on his favorite chair, baby wipes strewn down the hallway, a Johnny jump up blocking his escape to the bathroom. He would pick up Howling Baby, who would wail louder, poop and get snatched from his hands by teary Mommy. He would dream of leaving, even if for an extended research project in the Sahara.

Proud little world travelers.

I was not going to let Mommy wreck my world. I was going to go to war-torn and wild places to live in huts and do great things to make God happy. And if I had a husband, he was going to have to run to keep up.

I used to think this, and then I found a tiny human being living inside me.

■   ■   ■

"There's a lump the size of a grapefruit in my abdomen," I croaked one fateful morning. Tears puddled my eyes. "Feel it," I told Adam. "It's either a baby or a tumor."

Adam set down the bucket he'd just used to bathe himself in the dirty water of El Porvenir, the Nicaraguan mountaintop village where we had lived for a year. We were back visiting Nicaragua for just a couple weeks, then flying back to the United States to switch luggage and head out forty-eight hours later to live in Lanzhou, China, the city *Time* had named "the most polluted city in the world." Every day in China would hold a mix of teaching English, leading Bible studies, riding jam-packed buses and eating burn-your-lips-off Chinese food. We had no insurance for another two weeks, and even then we didn't know if it would cover this pre-existing "condition" and thought it likely that my job and graduate-school scholarship would be canceled if I tried to take time off work. This was no time to have a tumor. Or a baby.

Adam sat down on the cot next to me and pressed his hands into what should have been a bit of extra blubber from all the rice and beans I had been eating. His hands met a solid mass, bigger than a softball.

The nearest health care clinic was hours away on foot, and we were not leaving the village for three days. "Let's just not think about it until we can get down the mountain," he tried to reassure me. "We can have Sue check this out." Our friend Sue was a nurse, another American living with her family in Nicaragua, and we planned to visit them for Christmas later that week. "No use worrying about it until we can get it checked out by a doctor."

Right. As if that's possible for a woman who has just discovered a grapefruit in her abdomen.

Since being told by a doctor years ago that I would likely not have children, we had been married three-and-a-half years. My body never seemed regular, and we figured it would take a miracle for us to be pregnant, but it wasn't by any means a miracle I was asking for. Adopting later in life sounded fine. In the meantime, I liked our kid-free life.

We didn't know anyone with babies except people a decade older, mommy-types who carried diaper bags with little duckies and teddy bears and got mysterious thrills from holding their bug-eyed little lumps that barfed on their shoulders. Like most of my friends, I didn't do a good job of getting to know anyone outside my own life stage, so I didn't know what parenting would be like. Meanwhile I was probably unknowingly alienating a lot of other women like the Mommy-me I could imagine tied up in a closet.

A part of me desperately wanted to keep my full-time, free-all-the-time lifestyle. *Lord let this be a tumor—a big benign tumor,* I prayed. *Let us go into town, find a hospital, take it out and go on with life. Please, Lord, let it be a tumor.*

That didn't seem like what a person is supposed to pray. So in the evening, just after sunset while the village without electricity was already preparing for sleep, I sat down on the back porch of the barnlike building where we slept and stared out over the valley miles below. Adam was inside reading by candlelight, and I picked up my Bible to look for help. I had been meaning to read Genesis so I opened up to the first page and got as far as the first command God gives humans: "Be fruitful and multiply." Very funny, God.

What I wanted was an example of a good mom who managed to set aside whatever selfishness was making this so difficult for me. I started with Mary, the mother of Jesus. She wasn't ready to be a mom either. When I read the story of the angel announcing to her that she would have a baby, my eyes stuck on the words, "Mary was greatly troubled" (Luke 1:29). I bet. I had always pictured that lasting about ten minutes, and then Mary went back to being the perfect, pious lady ready to give up her fiancé, her honor and her whole life without an eye twitch.

Well, if Mary was anything like me, this terror was going to take a while longer. "Do not be afraid," the angel told Mary (Luke 1:30). Easier said than done. I closed my Bible.

Now there's something I need to explain about Nicaraguan weather. For over half the year, from around October until May, it simply does not rain on the west side of Nicaragua. Their dry season is dry. During the year we had lived in Nicaragua, I saw rain only once during the dry season, and it was a sprinkle in March when the rains were already on their way back. Now it was December, smack in the middle of the dry season. It simply does not rain in December.

I sat there on the stairs outside the barn, steaming with frustration over the mess my life had become. I wished I weren't so mad about this probable tiny baby in my belly that was supposed to cause me joy. I noticed a wind swishing through the dry trees. The night grew darker and the stars disappeared. I felt a cool touch on my toes. Drops fell, releasing tiny mushroom clouds of dust in the road. The soft, plunking sound of single drops grew to the steady hum of rain. Here on this mountain named El Porvenir—The Forthcoming—in the middle of the dry season, in the middle of nowhere, God sent rain.

In those raindrops God whispered to me, "Do you see now that I control the wind and rain and so much more? Do you see that I am in control of your life and this new life inside you? Do you believe now that I planned this because I love you?" Tears dripped down with the rain.

■　　■　　■

Three days later, on Christmas Eve, Adam and I said long goodbyes to our village friends and then made the five-hour bus trip to Sue's home in the city.

Their home was a perfect haven for weary travelers like us. Remembering Mary with a newfound fondness, I sat my frightened self down at their kitchen table and thanked God we weren't in a stable that night. Sue, her husband and their two elementary-school-age children were building gingerbread houses. They laughed and sang, the children drifted in and out of Spanish, and they told stories of the years they had spent traveling the world from Mozambique to Nicaragua, all as a family. Finally when the gingerbread homes sat carefully lined up on the table, I found myself alone in the kitchen with Sue. I told her about the lump.

Sue felt my abdomen and concluded, "It's likely just a benign tumor or cyst of some sort, since you don't seem to notice yourself feeling different." She wiped up some gingerbread crumbs from the table. "But we can get you a pregnancy test tomorrow. If that is a baby, you may even be two months along." *Two months*. My heart and mind raced.

The sun came up on Christmas Day, sweltering as usual. After fresh Nicaraguan coffee and breakfast, Sue rode off on her bike to a pharmacy. Half an hour later, Adam and I sat in a back bedroom staring at two little lines on a cardboard strip. "Let me see that package again," Adam said, even though we knew very well that two lines meant *embarazada*—pregnant.

"Do you think we could talk about this?" My voice cracked.

He sat down on the bed next to me. His words were slow, careful and some of the most beautiful I have ever heard. "I suppose I haven't wanted to think about this for the last week because I was afraid." He reached for my hand and gave it a reassuring squeeze. "I was afraid because if it's true, and we're going to be parents, I'd be so happy. I didn't want to think how crushed I'd be if it turned out *not* to be true."

My brain spun. This was a complete one-eighty. *Crushed if it weren't a baby? Happy if it was a baby? You could be happy for a baby, even in our circumstances, even for all the changes it would bring?* Did Adam know how many times babies woke up in a night and how hard it is to type while you're holding a baby and how much car seats cost? Probably he didn't know about any of that, but he was right about the happy part. God's words to Adam and Eve, "Be fruitful and multiply," were a blessing, not a curse. And when God tells us to do something, God shows us how.

When we came out of the guest room and said, "We're pregnant," Sue threw her arms up high, danced around the table, sang out "Praise God!" and hugged us both. My eyes welled up again at the sight of someone praising God for how he had crumbled my life plans.

The next day Sue directed us to an ultrasound clinic where a nurse fired up her machine and stuck a little microphone thing on my abdomen. She rambled on about head circumference, femur lengths, that this was a little girl. . . . We just stared—at the screen, at the woman, at each other. A tiny body with kicking legs and arms danced on the screen. A baby. Our baby. Our *baby!*

Adam paid for the ultrasound, flabbergasted at the price of just $10.25—a godsend for a young couple without insurance. Only when we walked back outside did Adam stop to think out loud, translating what the tech had said. "*Dieciocho y media semanas . . .* eighteen-and-a-half weeks—over four months?! We're halfway through this pregnancy!"

Our questions then could have filled a book: What would our families say? Could we still go to China? Where would this little girl be born? How would we pay for the medical bills? What would we name her, in just five months? Right now though we just laughed, hugged, shook our heads and stood blinking at each other.

■　　■　　■

Children, it turned out, were not at all as life-wrecking as we imagined. We named our daughter Phoebe after a woman of God who traveled and helped the church (Romans 16:1). We still went to China and both finished graduate school. We kept making intentional time for dates to keep parenting from consuming our marriage. We discovered that newborns are remarkably like purses: they are easy to carry around, and they don't care a bit about culture shock, new languages or different homes as long as you hold them. We never owned a crib, and Phoebe slept on hotel floors, restaurant tables and bus seats. She rode along wherever we went, bright-eyed, curious and babbling in the baby sling I made. Our Chinese neighbors doted on her, as did our South African neighbors on her little brother, Zeke, born two years later. Eventually the kids would carry their own little backpacks in the airport, make puppets out of empty airsickness bags and whatever else they found en route, and invent words in Zulu, Chinese and Spanish. Phoebe had no car seat for five of the first six years of her life, and in her first eight years we lived in fourteen homes. We didn't let them slow us down, and they always returned the favor.

Children will lead us into Amazing Days if we let them.

Our children initiated many Amazing Days. Having kids with us around the world not only shaped Phoebe and Zeke for the better but also shaped the difference we made as a family. Their presence opened doors for friendships and put people at ease in crosscultural situations. My first friendship with a Zulu woman happened because she worked on our landlord's property and brought her four-year-old daughter to work. The girl came to our house to play with Phoebe and Zeke while her mother worked. Sometimes we would walk a half mile down the road to visit that family. Sometimes the children played happily together as if oblivious that they shared only a few words in common. Other days the stress wore on them. One evening I got into an important conversation at this family's house and didn't realize the sun had nearly set until my children, hungry and worn out, went into meltdown. Phoebe collapsed on the ground in a temper tantrum, and Zeke, just over a year old, refused to let me set him down. My Zulu friend insisted that what they needed were good spankings. Feeling more inept than ever at explaining our cultural differences, I said an awkward fast goodbye, dragged Phoebe to her feet and set out walking. After a few more whining complaints, Phoebe sniffled and asked me to tell a story. For the rest of the walk home, step by three-year-old-sized step, I wove imaginary stories about children like them in foreign countries with wonderful friends and adventures.

Days like these reminded me that children are just humans after all, and small humans at that. They need extra care and attention when they're being stretched, but just as for adults, that doesn't mean they shouldn't ever be stretched. We bonded as a family as we relied on each other through car breakdowns, delayed airplanes and new communities. As we helped them process what they saw in life, we benefited also by having to clearly articulate our beliefs. We wrestled always with wisely discerning what was best for our family as a whole without straying toward fretting over every detail of our children's lives. And our children constantly forced us to slow down and see what was in our path. On that long walk home from our neighbor's house when all I wanted was to rush home and set down Zeke at our long-awaited dinner table, we still had to stop and bend down to look when Phoebe spotted sparkly pebbles along the roadside.

When we moved from the countryside to a city in South Africa, our children were quick to spot the big double arches of McDonald's, the magical place their grandparents had introduced them to during a month back in the United States. Every time we drove past McDonald's, three-year-old Zeke would attempt to amaze me with his letter-reading intelligence by shouting "M! McDonald's!" He never read any other *M*'s. I supposed children somehow inherently love McDonald's—the shiny things, the playground, the salty food, the shouting and jumping and screaming.

So we caved in and went. Adam and I conspicuously ordered takeout food from the Indian restaurant next door, but we went the whole nine yards and bought Happy Meals for the kids. It was pure bliss.

The thing that made me love our life wasn't that they ate all their Chicken McNuggets, or that they climbed all over the playground, or anything McDonald's expects kids to like at their restaurant. It was that Phoebe took her Happy Meal box and carefully tucked inside everything on the table: the plastic cup from a side of corn (yes, they offer a choice of corn or French fries in South Africa), the toy, the plastic bag from the toy, the piece of paper giving choking warnings about the toy and the straw. She talked about every item as she placed it inside: "I think I could put things in this bag. And I can wash this straw and use it again. And I think I could color on this paper . . ." She decided not to keep the French fry bag because it was paper and would "probably tear if you put rocks in it or something."

Two days later they were still throwing their McDonald's balloons around the house while Adam laughed out loud. Perhaps our kids had been deprived of a few things by most North American standards, but they were beautiful little people in their deprivation. They were teaching us to see each day like Phoebe's Happy Meal— full of endless wonder and possibility (even at McDonald's).

■　　■　　■

Not that that lesson was always an easy one to learn. Picking up new identities as parents wasn't all jolly and easy. When we found out we would be parents, Adam entered a serious growing season of figuring out what it meant to be a dad. A year later, I would still fume when people greeted our baby without so much as a nod to us, or when friends stopped inviting us out because baby's bedtime was eight o'clock. How many times I wanted to scream at somebody, "Parents are people too!"

As parents, we came face to face with the fact—true for everyone, but often ignored—that we are not the center of our own universe. When we returned from China and Zeke was born, we hunted for jobs in what I believed *had* to be our next continent: Africa. The job openings we kept finding were in warring or sweltering hot places that we realized just would not work for a family with a newborn and a two-year-old. Every door to Africa was closing, and only one door stood wide open: a job opportunity for Adam as a residence hall director at the University of Wisconsin–Oshkosh. "Oshkosh" brought to mind OshKosh B'gosh bib overalls, a truck factory, flat dull land and probably flat dull people. The weekend Adam accepted the job in Oshkosh, I couldn't talk about the job without crying. Our new home was a residence hall from the 1970s with industrial blue carpet everywhere, no land for a garden, a streetlight glaring through our windows and a whole lot of Caucasian neighbors. I wanted to finally get to Africa, the countries and cultures I'd been called to for years. Instead, I was moving to a place I would never choose to live.

A few weeks after we arrived in Oshkosh, we went to a new members class at a church we'd started attending. The first day, we filled out a worksheet designed to help us identify what spiritual gifts each of us had and to discuss how we might use those gifts in our church and community. Of all the gifts on the inventory, I came out dead last in one called "helps." "Helps," the guide explained, meant doing routine tasks to free others to do the ministry God called them to do. It is often done behind the scenes, without looking for recognition, with an attitude of humility and service. That sounded like a perfect description of my whole life right now as a full-time mom: behind the scenes, unrecognized, all about helping some other unappreciative little diaper-clad trolls grow up to do what God wants *them* to do. And I could not be less gifted in it.

One night on our first week in the apartment, baby Zeke woke me up and I found myself unable to fall back asleep. I sat in our living room and poured out complaints and questions to God for the hundredth time. Why did you weigh me down with a concern for poverty and people far away if only to bring us here? Why do I seem to be wasting what I'm good at and floundering around stuck doing what I don't feel good at?

As I walked back to the bedroom, a tiny motion caught my eye from a corner of the kitchen window. I stopped to look closer and noticed a spider. Her legs and web sparkled in the streetlight as she carefully wove her web, a process I realized I had never in my life stopped to watch. I found myself more awed with every new strand she placed.

This watching, this recognizing of the beauty in God's creatures, I realized, was what I needed more than I needed any certain place. I had asked to go to a land of elephants and "big things," things unmistakably screaming messages of God's diverse beautiful work and people's reliance on him. Instead he brought me to a place with common old kitchen window spiders. My job was to learn to notice that these, right here in front of me, were his, and so was my life, even in Oshkosh, Wisconsin.

■   ■   ■

Even as I stood watching the spider, words came back to me from a few months earlier. Just before Zeke was born, I visited a monastery for a weekend retreat. There I listened as a monk explained to visitors why they live in a monastery.

"God draws a circle around every one of us," he said. "Some people have big circles, some people have smaller ones. My circle is right here in this monastery, but I promise you, even loving people here is a tough enough job. We pray for people outside this little circle too—we can always pray. Your circle may be small or large, near or far from where you began. Your job is always the same: love the people in that circle."

My circle for that year was Oshkosh. I found it not too small at all. I got introduced to a Sudanese family and visited them weekly for some English practice while our children played together. I volunteered as a mentor for a crisis pregnancy center. A friend offered to share her garden with me. Our families started a Bible study together, and our children became best buddies. God knew the timing of when he wanted us in Africa, and he knew when we needed to be in our little circle in Oshkosh.

I know friends in circles who really hurt. Some are wishing for a spouse or a child. Some wish to be done with school, or done paying off loans, or done caring for a relative. Some wish they weren't locked into school loan payments, houses that won't sell, jobs that hardly pay. Some wish they weren't growing old while their dearest dreams gather dust in an attic of their memory. Some wish life were more exciting, more neatly fit together, more rewarding and more glorious.

In every circle, there is enough of God.

Children are one of life's biggest reminders that we have circles around us. We have limits. We are limited in what we can accomplish in a lifetime, limited in our control over another human's life, limited in how well our brain works (especially on four hours of sleep), limited in physical and emotional endurance, limited in days and hours and minutes.

I still have my moments of wishing I were in other places, but now it's not because I'm trying to escape some Mommy threatening to tie the real me in a closet. The Mommy *is* me, and I wouldn't be happier as anyone else. When I stop to see where my life has led, I marvel at how God gave me unique gifts that he lets me put to use as a mother. As Mommy, I get to sing songs with my children, memorize all the countries in the world, build castles out of cardboard, make up stories and songs, and pray by name for our friends around the world. Sometimes I still feel like my skull will crack from too many hours answering questions about photosynthesis, mediating fights and gluing googly eyes on sock puppets. But when the end of summer comes, the Mommy in me starts feeling my heart will crack for missing these little people all through the school day.

I am glad I don't get everything I ask for.

ORDINARY ADVENTURES
for Parents

- Climb a tree.
- Invent a game.
- Project a movie on the wall and invite friends.
- Go on a nighttime hike or play tag by a streetlight.
- Plant seeds together.
- Go fishing.
- Put a map on the wall and mark people and places to pray for (find resources at www.operationworld.org).
- Hold a lemonade stand for a good cause.
- Visit a retirement home.
- Make more babies.

10

THE REVOLUTION

COMMUNITY
Chrissy

As we climbed into the car on a Tuesday night, Phoebe looked up at the dark clouds oozing across the sky. In a voice on the verge of tears, she whimpered the question on all our minds: "Is it going to rain?"

By the time we reached the end of the driveway, the sky had provided the answer: yes. Big drops splattered across the windshield. Another Tuesday night family sports group doomed.

The previous summer, our first back in the United States, we had signed the kids up for a few community sports. We soon discovered that in a city the size of Madison, especially when you have just moved in, community sports don't necessarily feel like community. For weeks, I watched the games, never holding a single conversation with anyone along the sidelines, until one week I made up my mind to strike up a conversation with just one person, whoever sat next to me. I discovered that the woman in the lawn chair next to me actually lived in our neighborhood, but their son was older than Phoebe and Zeke, and on a different baseball team. Their lives were busy, our kids were the wrong ages, and neither of us suggested exchanging phone numbers.

Phoebe's baseball coach often showed up late and offered little to no coaching to the fifteen kids on her baseball team. Zeke dripped sweat as he chugged back and forth on the soccer field, usually ten feet behind the ball and behind the couple of boys on his team a year older and a foot taller. Frustrated that our kids seemed neither to improve in sports skills nor to have much interest in the games, we succumbed to the disturbing urge to shout at our kids from the sidelines so they would beat out (or maybe even beat up) some other little kids.

This didn't seem right.

So this second summer back in the United States we dreamed up another plan. We invited a few families we had come to know in the neighborhood to join a once-a-week family sports night. Parents would play along. We would involve kids of any size and ability. We would get to know people in our own neighborhood. People said it sounded like a great idea, so we set up an email list, chose a date to start and showed up.

Hardly anyone else did. We had to cancel a few weeks because of bad weather. Other weeks we canceled when no one came. A few weeks we managed to make teams for kickball or capture the flag out of just a couple families. Our kids couldn't help but notice that this wasn't quite what it was supposed to be.

So when the rain came down on yet another Tuesday night, the tears dripped down the little faces in the back seat. My phone rang— I assumed someone calling to say they wouldn't be coming. Maybe we could turn around.

"Are you coming?" asked Doug, a new friend from the neighborhood who had brought his family to nearly every sports night so far.

"We were going to, but . . ."

"We're coming!" the dad of the other faithful family announced into the phone and hung up before I had a chance to finish.

Eight minutes later, our two families were at the park, climbing out into the pouring rain, throwing Frisbees and splashing barefoot in puddles. Ultimate Frisbee, it turns out, works just fine with three-year-olds in the field of play, even in pouring rain. We invented new rules that worked for our small teams and young age range. We shouted and cheered when six-year-olds caught Frisbees, dads leapt into the air to catch passes in end zones, and the three-year-olds ran in the right direction. We played until everyone was shivering, then stood in puddles and laughed and talked some more, then drove home to write "Frisbee with kids in rain" straight onto the Amazing Days list. These were days and friends we would remember for the rest of our lives.

Two weeks later, when Doug's family was out of town, we arrived on Tuesday night to find ourselves the only ones at the sports field again. That week, we gave up. We sent out an email admitting we would have to end the Tuesday night sports group. We couldn't go on driving to a field hoping, waiting and letting down our kids. Friends wrote back saying the group had been a good idea, that they wished it had worked, that they were sorry, but that they just got too busy.

■　　■　　■

Which is what we all so easily get—busy with too many things. In eighteen months back in the United States, we had invited over dozens of people but could name only a couple families we had found time to see more than once. We had slowly made a lot of acquaintances. Very few were close buddies who would just stop by unannounced, who would help make major life decisions, who would trust us to watch their kids at a moment's notice or be at home when we needed someone to laugh at the latest messed-up haircut. We were tired of a few dozen sprouting acorns of potential future friendships, and ready for at least a few strong oak tree friendships.

We knew people who lived in the United States in well-connected communities. Some friends lived in cul-de-sacs where neighbors got together every month for potlucks and shared neighborhood babysitting clubs and even knew each other for years before they chose to move onto the same block. Others met every Friday to play cards or every Sunday for lunch or every Tuesday for Zumba. Others checked in daily through texts and Facebook and even stopped by unannounced.

A spontaneous attempt at "sand dune sledding" with friends in South Africa

Living overseas we were often wowed by community. It's not that everyone from my own subculture is bad at community and everyone else around the world is good at it, but I find I have a lot to learn from people who didn't grow up with the individualist mindset I did. In Nicaragua we could always find gatherings of men and women out lingering in the center of town talking. No one ever complained if we dropped in for a surprise visit any time. They would usher us to sit down on a bench, rock, bucket, hammock or whatever they had to sit on, pull out some food even if only a day-old toasted tortilla, and welcome us into the home. In China we first experienced the bonds of a team of expats. In South Africa, long before we spoke more than a phrase of Zulu, we'd been hugged and fed and welcomed to a Zulu church, and later we would make lifelong friendships with white South African families who invited us to camping trips, weekly moms-and-kids gatherings, Bible studies and *braais* (barbecues). Back in the United States, a Zulu professor I met in the first months we were living in Madison surprised me on my first visit to his office by inviting our whole family over for dinner with his family.

A Kenyan woman once told me, "If I don't see my neighbor in a day, the day is not done." On one morning while I stayed with a family in Kenya I counted nine separate people who stopped by the home before 8:00 a.m. They brought eggs or left with a cup of milk from the family cow, and they carried rolled-up bundles from other morning errands. No doubt some came to set eyes on my white face, but even if a four-eyed Martian spent a weekend at our home in the United States, I doubt we would have nine visitors stop by all day, let alone before 8:00.

We had been fortunate to experience close-knit community in the past both overseas and in the United States, but we were finding it harder than ever now. The question we faced was, what happens to the rest of us who haven't fallen into one of those tight groups yet? How does community get started where none seems to exist?

■   ■   ■

Back in college when I was tacking up signs in the dormitory bathroom, a young woman named Patricia would sometimes perch on the bathroom windowsill hugging her knees and keeping me company. We would talk about the crazy concepts we came across in classes—ideas like sheep farming, the South African Truth and Reconciliation Commission, community supported agriculture or explanations for why a billion people in the world lived in extreme poverty. We held in common a burning desire to run away and *do* something about all the issues we were learning about but couldn't touch.

So we kept talking. We decided to meet every Tuesday night in my dorm room to talk about whatever from our classes was exploding in our minds. We would invite other people who were equally brimming with questions and inspiration. Adam was the first person invited, and others soon joined. We called the group "The Revolution." (Adam gets more excited when things are branded. And when Adam is excited, he gets other people excited.)

At The Revolution, we talked of books and classes and future possibilities and the meaning of life. One week a friend shared about desertification in Africa; another time we processed theories of economic development for Latin America. Some nights we read about Gideon or Nehemiah; some nights we prayed loudly into the night. We began sharing a meal of plain rice in solidarity with hungry people around the world (and to stretch our meager budgets while having more time to talk). In one hard topic after another, we kept coming back to the phrase, "Jesus is the answer." We were reading the Bible, that revolutionary handbook, and talking about it together. It was an incubation time. We learned that humans do our best at incubating idea eggs when we huddle together a little. Like penguins.

From those who attended The Revolution, several spent time volunteering around the world after graduating. Today one man is a lawyer with a prestigious firm in Washington, D.C. One is a public health nurse. One spent a year working with Mother Teresa and nearly became a nun. One cares for people with disabilities. Another leads a prayer movement and helps people caught in human trafficking in her city. One builds schools in Sudan. I doubt any of us would be the people we are today if it weren't for those formative days hashing out ideas and dreams together.

We called our group The Revolution because we talked about the revolutionary lives we wanted to live outside the meetings, but in a sense, the community of that group was in itself revolutionary. In a society where we can neatly tuck ourselves away behind computer screens and garage doors and talk face to face with other human beings less than once a day, community *is* revolutionary.

■   ■   ■

Much of what we learned about community we learned in the first summer we were married while we lived at a thirty-year-old Christian service community in Georgia called Jubilee Partners. All thirty or so short- and long-term volunteers, including college students, families, children and retirees, lived on Jubilee Partners' five-hundred-acre property. The property included single-family homes, duplexes, multifamily homes and dormitory-style rooms. Every weekday, we ate lunches and dinners together on long wooden tables in a community building and took turns cooking, cleaning and washing dishes. Everyone worked various jobs on the property. Some days included maintaining the community's huge garden, blueberry patches, fruit orchards, chickens, cow and goats. Other days we'd be teaching English or driving to doctor appointments or grocery shopping with the families of refugees who also stayed for a few months at a time on the property in homes of their own. The community held a church service to-

gether on Sunday nights, optional prayer times before work in the morning and devotional times after lunch. Sometimes we needed those prayer times to keep from pulling each other's hair out. Or worse.

Community, we learned, has its challenges. Someone mixes up bread dough and leaves it to rise over the edge of the bowl and all over your teaching notebook. Someone laughs that oh-so-annoying donkey-sounding laugh every five minutes on the community landline when you're trying to sleep. Someone eats all the blueberries you picked and saved for your breakfast. Someone heard a refugee family's story of pain and loss and needs to wonder aloud how God can watch so much evil going on in this world.

The view from the door of our church in South Africa in a round room of someone's house. Church doesn't have to be fancy.

We also learned that community is worth all the challenges. Without busy commitments outside the community, we had time to spend together. Some nights we stayed up late talking in the big community building that had no cell phones, no Internet and no television. Other evenings we spent drinking Coke, eating Oreos and talking over card games with the families of Kosovar refugees who came there to learn English. As we washed dishes by hand, picked acres of blueberries, dug up thistles, hung laundry, grafted apple trees or walked through the forest on the way to the refugee school building, we exchanged life stories, hopes, fears and dreams.

■   ■   ■

On one afternoon at the end of our first summer at Jubilee Partners, I sat reading outside the building where we lived. The sun was setting, and the tall grasses along the edges of the yard were speckled with yellow and purple flowers. Adam and I lived in a building with four small apartments. Next to us stayed Jorge and his wife, Dalia. They had moved there from their home in Nicaragua to spend a few months volunteering and studying English before they took seminary classes in Indiana. It was the first time I had lived beside Spanish speakers. I found it exhausting pulling out the few bits of the language I had learned in school. Jorge and Dalia both politely managed to make some sense of my fumbling misconjugated two-word sentences, but by the end of our conversations I always felt my cheeks were sore from forcing myself to smile. On this afternoon, Jorge and Dalia were sitting in rocking chairs on the other side of the veranda speaking in Spanish.

Out of the corner of my eye, I noticed Dalia stand up, pick up a bicycle, stretch her leg over it and wobble forward, tippy toes on the ground. She offered a nervous grin to her husband, he laughed, and I understood what was happening. This forty-year-old woman had never ridden a bicycle.

She pushed forward, lifted both feet to the pedals and began rolling down a hill, wobbling sharply left and right, squealing all the way. Twenty feet later she tipped to one side and crashed, catching most of her weight on one foot and then slowly collapsing sideways with the bike on top of her. Jorge and I both jumped to our feet. Dalia lay on the ground laughing too hard to speak.

Jorge was rolling in laughter now too, and soon so was I. Together we helped Dalia to her feet and each held a handle bar to steady her before she slowly rolled down the hill. When she crashed, we propped her up and laughed some more, again and again.

Dalia did not learn to ride a bike that day. I did, however, learn that it's worth getting out of a chair to create a bit of community, even when it's a frightening, stretching community where we hardly even know how to communicate. Later in the summer, this family would connect us to an organization they had worked with in Nicaragua, and through that connection, fourteen months later Adam and I would move to El Porvenir. There I would find myself replaying this experience a thousand times over in new variations. Instead of getting out of my seat to laugh alongside a woman learning to ride a bike, I would be leaving my room to walk with Yaya to her bean field, sloshing water all over myself as women taught me to carry buckets of water on my head, visiting a woman's house to see if she wanted to practice reading, always overcoming that same inertia in order to get out and interact with someone.

Whether in an intentional community, in Nicaragua or here in Madison, it's the same story of overcoming inertia.

■　■　■

The seven-year-old boy in the Frisbee-playing family asked me recently, "Wouldn't it be great if your best friend lived right down a hill from your house and you could just get on your bike and coast down without even pedaling?"

"Do you have a best friend like that?" I asked, perhaps just a little jealous if the answer was yes.

"No," he admitted. "But wouldn't it be *great?*"

It would be. That's just what I want: a downhill easy automatic road to a friend's house. Somebody I can see three times a week, or even three times a day, who isn't weirded out by friends coasting on in without an invitation.

Even if we want community, it's rarely a downhill coast to get there. Community takes some bravery and intentionality, some feeling like a fool, some sacrifice, some forgiving when other people are jerks and some apologizing when I'm a jerk.

United States dominant culture over the last centuries has taken plenty of hard hits against the kind of community my ancestors could have had just by going about their lives trading eggs, borrowing thread and plows, or hanging around the corner grocery store deciding whether it would rain on the hay. Since the Industrial Revolution, people have become ever more disconnected from their economic base, and that leads to disconnection from a close-knit community. People follow jobs to cities where no one knows them, much less their grandparents and second cousins. In a book about American pioneers moving from rural to urban settings in the early 1900s, I found one character's description of his city life hauntingly similar to our own experience back in the United States:

Freedom so often means that one isn't needed anywhere. . . . Off there in the cities there are thousands of rolling stones like me. We are all alike; we have no ties, we know nobody, we own nothing. When one of us dies, they scarcely know where to bury him. Our landlady and the delicatessen man are our mourners, and we leave nothing behind us but a frock coat and a fiddle, or an easel, or a typewriter, or whatever tool we got our living by. All we have ever managed to do is to pay our rent, the exorbitant rent that one has to pay for a few square feet of space near the heart of things. We have no house, no place, no people of our own. We live in the streets, in the parks, in the theaters. We sit in restaurants and concert halls and look about at the hundreds of our own kind and shudder.[9]

Chilling, but a familiar echo. Today we work more hours in a week than ever, and more than ever time is money. We rush and bustle, pack in more activity and stop stopping by. We drive across town to the big store with everything except people we know, because megastores offer lower prices than little bitty stores. We value efficiency, and for efficiency in communication there's nothing slicker than posting and messaging for not just one but a thousand "friends" at a time. With no time left to visit our friends' homes, we stave off boredom with Netflix or the infinite trinkets of the Internet. Surely we can find a thousand ways to save time and therefore save money. In the process, out goes community as God seems to have intended it. We forget how to treat people as people, how we need people to make us people. In heaven, I've heard it said, we will walk on gold and love people. On earth, we more often love gold and walk on people.

Ultimately community requires that I choose to value another person, even when it means giving up something of myself. Community requires making room for someone else's needs and emotions. In Nicaragua, it meant opening the door to girls asking me to teach crocheting

Adam gets ready for a three-legged race at the seminary where we taught in South Africa. Community requires tying ourselves to others.

at six in the morning when all I wanted to do was bathe and get a few minutes alone. In the United States, when I invited Phoebe's Girl Scout

Brownie Troop for a camping night in our yard, a girl asked me to lend her a pillow. Pretty soon four other girls wanted pillows, and I awkwardly drew the line. Then the first girl with the borrowed pillow got a bloody nose in the night all over my pillow. That's the kind of thing we sign up for when we go for community.

Without community, though, we tend toward deterioration. I see plenty of stories unfold like this: A person goes through an earthquake-to-the-worldview change, like accepting God's grace, or (to a lesser degree) a first dip in a foreign culture, or a statistic on how many young people get trafficked every year. His jaw hangs slack, he frantically blogs and shouts to the world, his heart pounds with what must be a lifelong conviction, and he proclaims, "I will never be the same!"

Then he goes home.

Months pass. He finds a thousand other ways to spend his time. His passion fades like the memory of last month's grocery list. He always has a channel of outstretched arms tugging him away from what truly matters. Some tugs offer nice logical reasons; some bring lousy reasons. If he wants to push through, he needs help.

That's where community comes in. We need like-minded, knit-together people living for Jesus. That's what church is made to be. The church is where we get together with people who believe the same kinds of things we do to remind each other that we're not crazy (or that we're crazy in good ways). Sure, in the church we'll find people who rain on our passion parade and give those sideways glances that say they really do believe we're crazy in not good ways. Fine, so they're in their own place along a journey, and not everyone is learning just the same thing I'm learning right now. If I look at the global church—the people spread all across the globe following Jesus and being his lips and lungs and fingertips around the world—I find no shortage of people who inspire, understand and even like me. It's worth finding a local church—a group I can see a few times every week who I can join with in a warm petri dish for growing inspiration. God wired us to need that kind of unity, and in a crazy sort of way, even God needs unity. We worship an incredibly unique God: three separate but unified persons of God the Father, Jesus and the Holy Spirit. This is a God who at his core is all about unity.

Dietrich Bonhoeffer in his book about community, *Life Together*, stresses that community will not fulfill every idealistic dream of emotional bliss and harmony. When a community instead deals with the disillusionment of being a bunch of imperfect people, that community, "with all its unhappy and ugly aspects, begins to be what it should be in God's sight, begins to grasp in faith the promise that is given to it."[10] As a community of believers we live out the reality God created us to live. We all need a revolutionary community.

My friend Vanessa wrote her master's thesis on how church communities can support single moms. Since then I've noticed how we're all in different ways walking around as broken families. Without a community, we try to meet all our own needs or all the needs of the people closest to us, when really none of us has everything we need. God gives us more sisters, brothers, moms, dads and cousins to complete our family needs.

No one should have to learn to ride a bicycle alone, and no one should have to live without community. When in the year after we returned to the United States I felt like I would do anything to escape the dark little cave of our home where I was shriveling up, I had to keep reminding myself that this desire, uncomfortable as it felt, was steering me in the right direction. God made all of us to get out of our caves. If I lose that desire, something has gone very wrong. If I stay away from people so long that I stop craving honest conversation or stop looking people in the eye, I'm burying my natural needs. I become like an anorexic believing she's fat when in fact she's starving. Without community, whether we recognize our hunger or not, we starve. The ancient Greeks had a word for those who just lived for the "id," for themselves. They were called "idiots."

■   ■   ■

Soon after we moved into our Madison apartment, I noticed that every time I went shopping at Target I turned into the Angry Target Lady.

I could walk into the store with my two kids all bubbly and thrilled to get to ride in the bright red cart and jam their knees next to each other and hang their heads out sideways looking upside-down at the tall stacks of plastic shoe racks and closet organizers. But before I'd chosen the first bottle of shampoo, they would become the Attention Deficient Target Kids and I would morph into Angry Target Lady. I said things I never thought I'd say. I shouted from halfway down aisles useless demands like, "Just quit crying and be *quiet,*" and "Phoebe get your feet in the cart or they'll get ground up in the wheels of this cart and that will *really* give you a reason to cry."

While I deliberated over baskets and closet organizers, my children's minds were turning to silly putty. Zeke kicked at a shelf full of glass candleholders. Phoebe yanked his arm and twisted his elbow. When we maneuvered our cart bulging with broom and mop handles and long plastic under-bed storage tubs into the checkout line, I spent my last ounce of patient-voice. I bent down to their level to say, "Now look, these things here are nice to see, right? But should we touch them?"

"No-no-no-no-no!" Zeke replied with a big head shake and a sing-song voice. I set the first stuff-holder on the conveyor belt for purchase, turned back for the second, and there was Zeke, finger extended, poking a banana. "Banana!" he said like an eighteen-month-old pronouncing the three syllables for the first time. He was four and knew better when he was not Attention Deficient Target Boy.

"Zeke!" growled Angry Target Lady. "Are you touching the bananas?"

His head nodded. "Yes-yes-yes-yes-yes."

The back of my neck ached and my eyes turned fuzzy and all the red circles started spinning like a tornado.

The kids went to the automatic door walking forward and

backward, making the door open and close while people dodged past them with purchases, wondering no doubt where their Angry Target Mom was. Where was I? Walking toward them shuffling through my cart realizing I forgot to put the bag of light bulbs and toothpaste into the cart. I turned back. "Kids, stay there," I shouted, not caring about the opening and closing doors. I walked past the first five checkout counters. I didn't recognize these faces. Oh Lord, I didn't have a clue where I checked out. How did I pay for my stuff and stuff-holders, hand someone a credit card, shuffle my children through the aisle and now not have any idea at all what my cashier looked like? Was it a woman or man? I was not sure. I dragged the Attention Deficit Target Kids away from cranking the candy machine handles. "Kids, come here. Come help me get our stuff back."

"Her nametag said Bethany," said Phoebe, always the reader with the photographic memory, sweetly running to catch my hand. Zeke pointed—"That one!" Sure enough, there was my bag. The cashier hadn't noticed it yet either. There in the big bright store, in my rush to grab my stuff and get home, I was so focused on my own little world that I became completely blind to another human being.

Way to go, Chrissy.

■   ■   ■

In Nicaragua when we got up early enough we would hang around talking to the old man Eliseo while he milked his cow and scooped out a couple cups of steamy warm milk for us from the bucket. In China we used to buy milk from a man who drove a bicycle around town with a huge milk can strapped on a rack over his back wheel. Twice a week, he stopped in our apartment courtyard and rang a cowbell. People came downstairs with their pots and bottles to fill. I had some of my best Chinese conversation opportunities during those minutes waiting our turn to place a container under the milk can spigot. When we finished, the milk man would tuck a cigarette in his mouth and pedal on to the next apartment building. I could look at this man and my neighbors and know without a doubt that these were all real people.

In South Africa, also, we got our milk from a farmer in our church who delivered milk jugs door to door twice a week. When we returned to the United States, Zeke sat eating his breakfast one day and suddenly wrinkled up his face in confusion. "Mama," he asked earnestly, "how did we get this milk?" To him the sequence of cow to farmer to bulk tanks to packaging to grocery store to checkout line was mystifyingly complicated.

It is to me too. I'm happy all the people along that chain of production have jobs. But I find it very easy to forget that they are real, human, a part of my life and worthy of my appreciation.

Inevitably I will buy milk from the grocery store in the United States. I will shop at Target. When I do, I'm learning to remember the names and faces of the people in the checkout lines and visit the same line each time. I now recognize the woman at the checkout whose mother has dining room walls painted the same color as my new curtains, and the man at the snack bar who has the names of his children tattooed on his arms. I hope to treat Bethany as a person with a name, a family, worries, dreams and a personality beyond her red shirt. I have also slowly identified favorite stores where people more often get treated like people. We found a post office where the guy behind the counter grew up a block from our house. He greets us by name and never rushes us through the line. We go to a hardware store with a discount for people from the neighborhood—not so much for the discount but because we like that they care whether or not we're local. They helped us choose rubber tubing to make a slingshot for the kids and gave Zeke a free cork to replace the one he'd lost from his pop gun. They carry water softener salt out to the car for us, and the walk is never far because the parking lot only holds four cars. We leave these places feeling more human and happier. (Maybe those are the same thing.)

Once when I walked through our neighborhood in Madison, I noticed an elderly woman standing outside in her socks talking to the mailman. The day was bright and sunny, I had nowhere to be in a hurry, and I took the first bold step. I talked to her. We chatted for a while there on the sidewalk and I learned that she was eighty-two years old and wonderfully friendly. Pretty soon I was stopping in whenever I walked by her house on the way to the grocery store. She would make coffee and give the kids popsicles and Gatorade while they petted her cat and we talked about life sixty years ago. Some days she was the only person I talked to during the long stretch of time when my kids were at school. Here was a person who was nearly always at home and who genuinely enjoyed spontaneous visits. To my surprise, she didn't seem to find it nearly so strange as I did that we had just struck up a friendship from scratch out of a conversation at her mailbox.

It's hard to make a very long list of Amazing Days without daring to enter into community. Many of our favorite Amazing Days have come from stretching our arms out wide to invite someone into our lives, or letting someone else surprise us with a welcome into their life. Some days it won't come easy. We'll invite and invite and never get invitations in return. I hated those weeks not knowing if anyone would arrive for sports night, waiting, hoping, apologizing to my kids when no one came. Still, I don't regret trying. When the group folded we continued seeing the family we tossed Frisbees with in the rain. We have even been known to stop by for surprise visits. If out of that attempted community sports night all we gained was one family of friends, it's still one more family of friends than we would have had if we stayed at home. Community is not a fast food I can pick up in a hurry. It's a slow food that requires time to simmer, but with a taste worth craving all my life.

ORDINARY ADVENTURES
in Community

- Have a potluck.
- Ask someone to teach you to knit, do carpentry, shop, garden, cut hair, debone chicken . . .
- Ride the bus.
- Invite people over to bake pizza from scratch.
- Read the whole New Testament out loud in one sitting.
- Take a vacation with some friends.
- Carpool.
- Stop by someone's house unannounced.
- Ask someone how they really are, take time to hear their answer, and check in with them a week later.

Putting on Underwear

FEAR
Chrissy

Life is not lost by dying; life is lost minute by minute, day by dragging day, in all the thousand small uncaring ways.

—Stephen Vincent Benét

We thought a story about a death would make a nice round ending for a book about really living.

But nobody died. And we're not complaining.

People pay attention when you start telling a near-death experience. When people get done reading my first book, *Into the Mud*, they nearly always say how touched they were by the story about taking little four-year-old Phoebe to a hospital in South Africa. Even Phoebe likes to hear the story. And when she hears us talking about it, she elbows us and whispers, "Tell about me getting sick in Kenya too."

So we tell about her getting sick in Kenya, because it's another near-death story and people pay attention. We were moving back from South Africa to the United States when we stopped in Kenya for a couple weeks to travel with a Kenyan friend. He took us to his home village, the same place I was visiting a year later when I raced along on the backfiring motorcycle with Mike. This first time all four of us went, and we stayed in the house of our friend's relatives, who gave us stinky, moldy cushions and several holey mosquito nets tied in every direction like a couple of lopsided pyramids over our family, and while we were trying to sleep on those stinky, buggy beds, Phoebe woke up and said, "I think I have a fever."

She did. She had a fever and kept on having a fever. We gave her doses from the little bottle of acetaminophen we'd brought, but the fever went higher, up past 105 degrees.

"Mama," she said, lying in the bed shivering the next morning, "I keep seeing a black line. I keep seeing a lady killing a horse where there should be a sheet. I'm scared."

Me too. I had never watched someone hallucinate. I called Adam, who was out with our Kenyan friend for the morning. I sat next to Phoebe, holding her hand until she drifted to sleep, and then I went into the room next door and cried.

Two days before, we had stayed at a church in a slum of Nairobi and our kids had run around barefoot in the pouring rain in mud puddles, giggling and laughing with some local kids. I wondered if, by allowing that cute photogenic moment with kids in a slum, I was responsible for this. My brain spun with terrible options. *She has yellow fever. She has malaria. She has typhoid. She has meningitis. She has hepatitis G or H or whatever they go up to now. She has some disease you get from swimming in water with snails or duck poop.*

I thought about losing my little girl, about being that missionary who has to give up her own kid on the mission field. I had heard it pointed out that God lost his only son on the mission field. I guess that was supposed to be a comforting thought, and I was supposed to find it comforting that Jesus rose from the dead and that everyone who believes in him can join him up in heaven for a big everlasting party. Mostly I just wanted Phoebe to be okay.

Our Kenyan friend sent a motorcycle taxi to come fetch us. With floppy Phoebe in my arms and Zeke up on the handlebars grin-

After the trip to the doctor, we enjoyed many more family motorcycle rides around Kenya.

ning, we sped off to the village's health clinic. The clinic was run by an old woman named Sister Teresa who looked like Mother Teresa and spoke in a cool German accent in Swahili and English and a few more languages she'd picked up during her fifty-three years in Africa. She looked in Phoebe's throat and let out a gasp, then shook her head a long time and said, "This girl has a very, very sick throat." She gave Phoebe antibiotics for septic tonsillitis and gave us a clean, quiet room to stay in. For the rest of our week we ate meals every day with Sister Teresa, savoring her wisdom collected over years of service, walking through the forests and gardens she had methodically nurtured out of bare soil, and getting to know the dozen orphaned kids who stayed with her. When Phoebe talks about Kenya she groans, "Ugh, I *hated* Kenya." She spent most of the week in bed feeling lousy as her body steadily recovered. When Adam and I think of Kenya we think of a beautiful place where God used a kind and faithful old saint to heal our daughter.

Why was Phoebe spared? I don't know. Why were any of us spared? Most of us could tell some story of nearly dying. For Adam it was when he crashed his car in high school. For me it was when in first grade I went into surgery for a congenital heart defect. In the middle of the surgery, my heart stopped beating. My dad says he remembers the doctor coming out of the operating room pale and shaken, long after he had expected to hear from him. The doctor explained, "We've never had this happen before. Her heart for some reason couldn't handle the surgery. Her heart stopped beating. We had some difficulty getting it started up again. There may be some brain damage."

Well, they did get my heart started up again, and here I am today. As far as I can tell, there was no brain damage (though Adam may disagree). I once was dead, but now I'm alive.

■   ■   ■

At the seminary in South Africa, we lived upstairs from a family from Rwanda. The wife was a seminary professor and the husband was working on his Ph.D. dissertation about what the Bible has to say on forgiveness. They invited us over for a generous meal, and as we set our napkins back onto the table after dinner, they agreed to tell us their story of escaping the genocide in 1994. We had asked before, and they had insisted it would take a good long evening to tell. The story was indeed worthy of a whole evening to tell. It unfolded like all the worst survival horror stories you can imagine: As a married couple of one Hutu and one Tutsi, they went into hiding as soon as the killing began, miraculously finding each other from separate cities where they worked and gathering their children from schools across the city. They spent days in hiding, hearing every day of more deaths, as one by one their friends and neighbors were being slaughtered, house by house, with the violence moving toward the place they were hiding. They set off walking, miraculously met an acquaintance with a vehicle, escaped to D.R. Congo, moved again to Nigeria and then again to South Africa.

When their story reached the present day, the wife concluded, "Every day I ask myself—what was I spared for? Is this—today—the reason I'm alive?"

It's a question worth asking. I like hanging out with people about twice my age because they face this question more often than most people my own age. I visited a Bible study at my parents' church. During the time to share prayer requests a white-haired man said he was going to have the battery in his pacemaker replaced later that week. "If that battery goes out," he said, "I go out. All I have to do is go into the doctor for about an hour and they fix it up, and I'm off and ticking for who knows how much longer. But it does make you think. I don't take much for granted anymore." His wife sat beside him smiling into his face and squeezing his hand.

It does make you think. Usually we don't know *what* it's supposed to make you think though. Death makes us think of walking through sanitized hospital hallways looking for the right room where someone we love is hooked up to tubes and beeping machines, or talking in quiet voices next to heaps of flowers in funeral homes. Thinking of death gives us the queasy feeling of sticking our nose near a bottle of bleach.

■   ■   ■

Soon after we moved back to the United States I found myself in a hospital, facing all those antiseptic smells and tubes and machines. I had been feeling a steady pain in my chest over a few days, and the urgent care clinic doctor decided with my history of heart issues, he couldn't do enough tests there to diagnose it. He sent me to the emergency room. I walked out of the clinic, realized I had no idea where the hospital was and turned around to ask for directions. I tried to repeat the directions back to the nurse. "You said right at the light? I mean, oh, left at the right, I mean, what?" I wasn't talking straight. Did I sound scared? Is a person supposed to sound scared when a doctor has just raised his eyebrows and said, "I recommend you go straight to the emergency room tonight"?

The waiting room was quiet when I entered the hospital. The triage nurse ushered me behind her desk where I explained my sore chest and my health history.

After a couple questions, the nurse excused herself to help a man with blood splashed on his T-shirt and his hand wrapped in a towel. He had stuck it under a lawn mower. His seven-year-old daughter stood next to him pacing. "Honey, it's gonna be okay," he told her, rocking and squeezing the towel. "Just don't look at it." The triage nurse wheeled him into a back room, and the girl stood looking lost. I wondered if I should go talk to her; she reminded me so much of Phoebe. The triage nurse returned just as the girl's mom showed up and sat holding her.

The nurse had nearly finished with my paperwork when another woman came in sobbing. Her face was red and blotchy and she cried, gasping for every breath. A guy in his twenties with a muscle shirt stepped up to the counter next to her. "She's having a really bad panic attack." He sounded disgusted and exhausted, puckering his lips and breathing out slowly. By the time the triage nurse was done with me, the man had left her. I sat next to her in the waiting room while she held a wad of tissues over her face and made little rhythmic sucking noises.

A nurse came to take me into a waiting room with a wheelchair— *a wheelchair.* I almost told the woman, "No, I can walk." Then I thought maybe she knew something I didn't know, so I rode. I imagined what I would say if I turned the corner and saw someone I knew. "I'm fine. This is all silly, really."

They left me in my room to wait for a doctor. I watched the disconnected heart monitor. The little break in the flat line slid across the screen, started again at the left, slid across again. *This is what it looks like to die.* A flat line. No life left. A woman next door was screaming, "I can't just do that! I got kids!"

Some more nurses came and went, and then the doctor, who listened to my heart murmur and said, "Yes, that's quite impressive for something benign." The nurses gave me a pill and a little cup of medicine that tasted like liquid toothpaste. Then they left me for what seemed like an hour. By now I had counted seven people, from clinic to hospital, whom I had told about my sore chest. It sounded dumb every time. I'm thirty-three. Only thirty-three-year-old hypochondriacs go to the emergency room for chest pain. Of course I'm not dying—people like me don't die, do they?

■　■　■

I remembered the phone call when my good friend in South Africa told me her HIV test had come out positive. She had two young boys near the same ages as my own children. I didn't know what to say. What I wanted to say was, "But you can't be dying. You're my friend." As if by virtue of being close to us, inside our own little circle, someone can't be dying.

I also remembered the first time I heard the wail of death. It wasn't in the United States, because most of us here don't wail over death, at least not outside in the streets where strangers hear it. It was in Nicaragua, while I was outside my friend Luz's house scrubbing a banana sap stain out of a pair of Adam's pants on a rock set up on a stick frame. I poured bowlfuls of water from a bucket onto the pants, rubbing on a bar of soap, trying to scrub up a lather, rinsing, getting nowhere, still hoping my Nicaraguan friends wouldn't come look over my shoulder and see how lousy I was turning out to be at hand washing. Then from over the hillside rose a sound like nothing I had ever heard from a human, like something wild, primordial. It was the sound of everything in a soul letting loose.

My friend Luz came racing out of her house, and in a few moments another woman, the source of the screaming, came tripping and stumbling down the hillside in her flip-flops, hair flailing behind her in tangles, tears streaming down her face. She ran into Luz's arms, laid her head on Luz's shoulder and wailed big rib-shaking sobs. There was nothing discreet and nothing quiet about it. At least fifteen other homes must have heard the lament. People peeked their faces outside or came to comfort the woman or gathered to talk in low voices.

I was the bumbling foreign idiot. *Quick*, my brain said, *do something kind and comforting. You're supposed to be the one helping poor people. Say something nice and Christian.* I stood glued to my laundry rock, completely without experience in how to handle a woman shrieking in the road because somebody died.

I later learned that the sobbing woman had seen her mother have a stroke and believed her to be dying, but in fact her mother soon recovered. I visited the woman's house a few months later when her daughter had just had a baby—right there in her bedroom. I found the new mom lying on a cot with a baby just a few hours old tucked up in blankets beside her. I had never heard the wailing mourning voice of death, and I had never seen a less-than-one-day-old baby either. Here in Nicaragua I was learning to face death and life, right out in the open, in little palm-roofed houses with dirt floors, one beside the other, for all to see.

■ ■ ■

As I write this chapter, it's autumn and my window overlooks fields of crumpled corn stalks, yellow walnut forests dropping leaves and dry prairie plants heavy with seeds bending slowly to the ground. Death is everywhere. I remember hearing a woman mention that every year when she sees chrysanthemum flowers she cries. Chrysanthemums mark the end of summer, the end of a season full of life.

I felt the same way about summer this year. On the Fourth of July, I sat on the porch of our newly rented home after dark watching some distant fireworks, wondering how it could be midsummer already. I had a printer to fix, Phoebe's Brownie Troop registration to send, students emailing me questions, a stack of bills, a desk too full to set a computer on, suitcases to unload, laundry to wash, peas to pick, spinach to freeze, groceries to buy, cakes to cook, long overdue vacuuming and a half-acre of weeds to pull. My to-do list always grew, never shrunk.

Earlier in the day I had snapped at Phoebe for some minor incident, and as she cried I realized my greatest fear was coming true—I was so distracted by stuff to do that I was wrecking our summer together. I wanted desperately not to just push a boulder up a hill every day or every week and watch it roll back down. I wanted more from life, and yet I kept falling back into the busy task-completing vortex. I wanted good days to go on without limit, from summer into infinity. What it really came down to was that I wanted not to die.

■   ■   ■

My friend Sarah, the artist who found her skin cancer at age twenty-nine, is one of the few people I know who thinks about death head on.

Within the span of four months, she went through two sets of skin cancer surgeries, a burst appendix plus emergency appendectomy with ensuing hellish recovery, and a suspicious breast lump. This came in the midst of caring for her first brand new baby and the accompanying sleep deprivation. For a time she felt very alone and disheartened because none of her friends knew how to talk about it with her.

"I used to beat myself up all the time," she admitted to me as we got our kids ready for a walk. "I would get to the end of the day and say 'Look at yourself. You haven't even gone outside all day and it's beautiful out.' But it became so real that just by going out in the sunlight I'm on my way toward basal cell carcinoma. It was like, all of a sudden I could die. And no one had prepared me for that."

She rubbed sunblock onto her cheeks and put on a wide-brimmed hat. "I know very well that there's no promise about how long we live. My husband could die in a car accident today. And I would hate that— you know, it's just nice having a husband and a dad for my kids and my dearest friend and partner and confidant and all that. It comes down to not wanting to suffer. I don't want to suffer." She lifted her younger son into a stroller, and added, "But who *does* want to suffer?"

I had no answer.

"People we call masochists," she answered herself and shrugged. "It's not as though wanting to suffer is a desirable trait. I used to roll these thoughts around in my head for days, weeks, months, even years, and what was always impossible to escape, and unfortunately not an encouragement, was that suffering was one of the things Jesus certainly *did* promise us. And it was difficult to find consolation in that. Because I just wanted the suffering to stop. But I don't think that's inherently wrong."

When thoughts of suffering and even death hit us smack in the face, we don't know what to do with them. We try to deflect them, but they leave little stains, little smudges all over us that show up as fears.

In the United States we put on fears every day as thoughtlessly as we put on underwear. We hardly notice our fears anymore because we've worn them so long. When we headed to South Africa, Adam and I saw kids bouncing on trampolines with gaping twelve-inch holes along the sides where a kid could drop into an eight-foot pit, and kids climbing fifty-foot trees, and kids spinning on the kind of merry-go-rounds that got banned from our playgrounds back when we were in elementary school. We watched those kids' parents quietly drinking tea from a distance while their children risked loss of life and limb, and we realized how fear-shaped our own society really is.

I'm not saying I want my kids playing with live wires hanging out of walls or chewing on pieces of glass picked up off the playground dirt. I do, though, want to stop and diagnose how much I have succumbed to the American epidemic of fear. In the United States we fear playgrounds, recalls, escalators, dogs, roller coasters, chicken meat, pesticides, water supply, air quality, gas prices, cell phones, immunizations, strip mining, inflation, dehydration, guns, gun control, climate change, stock market swings, swine flu, bird flu, unemployment, workaholism, stress, babies being born and, of course, death. What all these fears add up to is a big excuse to stay home, take no risks and care for yourself before anyone else.

My friend Sarah was right: Jesus is pretty clear on this one. You don't want to suffer? Too bad. "Take up your cross and carry it," said Jesus, and then he did just that. The disciples who followed him got murdered one after another. I can imagine a bunch of early Christians hiding in a cave somewhere, maybe just after Peter had joined the ranks of disciples getting killed, while somebody read aloud Peter's words: "Do not fear what they fear; do not be frightened. But in your hearts set apart Christ as Lord" (1 Peter 3:14-15 NIV 1984). When fear and danger set in, there's nothing easy about remembering that Christ's love is 100 percent assured at all times, and Christ is Enough with a capital E. We would rather make empty promises to ourselves like, "The safest place to be is in God's will." Plenty of God-following people prove that one wrong, if by safe we mean you won't break your nose or end up in the hospital or go without a job for three years or have your church burned down. Like Aslan, the Christ-figure lion in C. S. Lewis's *The Lion, the Witch, and the Wardrobe*, the deal with God is not safety. "Safe?" said Mr. Beaver describing Aslan. "Who said anything about safe? 'Course he isn't safe. But he's good. He's the King, I tell you."[11]

Maybe the reason many of us, even those of us who think we know God's love pretty well, still feel so afraid, is that we're working so hard to combat fears with the wrong tactics. Instead of dodging fears, we need to punch them in the face.

■　■　■

Prayer is like the superhero secret weapon designed perfectly to decimate fear. It is the single best tool for fear-fighting, and many of us never use it (and most of the rest of us don't use it well, including me most of the time). It helps to be specific. Not just, *God, help me not go crazy this summer*, but *God, help me get through this stack of stuff on my desk before breakfast. God, help both kids make at least one good friend this summer in our neighborhood. God, help Adam come home*

full of energy tonight to be present emotionally and physically with us.
God, help us plan out how to spend our weekend. God, help me get my
mind off myself and notice what you want to do with my life today.
God, help me and my family accept whatever the doctors say about my
chest pains with grace and courage.

If fears plague us like swarms of locusts, prayer is the industrial-
sized bug zapper. "Do not be anxious about anything," said Paul,
another one of those early Christians who knew how to conquer the
fear of death. "But in every situation," he went on, "by prayer and
petition, with thanksgiving, present your requests to God. And the
peace of God, which transcends all understanding, will guard your
hearts and your minds in Christ Jesus" (Philippians 4:6-7).

■   ■   ■

Sitting there waiting in the hospital for my chest x-ray and EKG results, I wondered how the lawn mower man was adjusting to the idea
of having less of a hand, and whether his daughter would have night-
mares. I wondered if the panic attack woman was drugged to sleep
now, and what I should have said to her, and if she'd go home any
better off than when she came.

I couldn't bring myself to fritter away time watching the television when I might be about to find out I was dying. I imagined a
tumor growing just beneath my sternum. I imagined multiple drug-
resistant strains of tuberculosis making snotty bubbles in my lungs.
I imagined a heart valve gone bad, not quite closing any more. I
imagined calling and canceling the class I was teaching. I imagined,
as I had on the motorcycle ride in Kenya, the end of any adventures,
not just overseas, but anywhere at all.

My hands were shaking. I figured it was most likely from hunger
and cold in the highly air conditioned room, but maybe also from
fear, or death coming on like a new phase, like a new home I would
have to move into.

I thought of all the times I had moved and not wanted to go. Of Adam convincing me to move to China, of the year in Oshkosh, of leaving our home in rural South Africa, of coming back and seeing that the new tenants had let the cabbages in my garden rot and the flower beds go to weeds. I thought of leaving Africa, the last big move.

Every time, the moves hadn't been as hard as I thought they would be. I remembered coming to China, where I thought I would hate the polluted city packed with four million people. The first week I was there, I discovered a rare patch of hundreds of acres of garden plots behind our college.

Adam and the kids do airport calisthenics during a long wait for a delayed plane.

I loved the sweet people who farmed there and sold their vegetables outside our apartment. They came to know me and baby Phoebe well. Even if I hardly understood their local dialect, I understood that God had given these neighbors and their gardens as a gift to me. Each time we have moved, I have found God had already prepared a place for me in ways I never would have imagined.

Jesus promised he would prepare a place for us after we die too. Some people don't want to talk about heaven because they think if we focus on heaven too much we'll get lazy, that heaven is just a cheap trick to make us not care what happens in life. I don't think so. I like knowing it's coming because it makes everything here a bonus. This life is extra. We don't have to fear here, because we are going home.

Scott, our friend and pastor, told a story about how the San Francisco Golden Gate Bridge was built. He said for a long time they were sending people out to work on it just balancing across narrow cables or planks, and people kept falling in the water and dying. As more people died, more people were scared, and the work went slower and slower. Finally progress seemed so slow that the bridge engineer decided they had to do something about the fears. He decided to spend over $130,000—the equivalent of over $1.5 million today—to stretch an elaborate safety net beneath the whole work area of the bridge. So they put up that net, the biggest the world had ever seen, and what happened? The workers zipped right along and finished the work in record time. Why? Because they weren't scared anymore.

Heaven is like that net. If I really know that a safety net is there, I can walk across the San Francisco Bay on a tightrope. Or I can endure car breakdowns and airplane delays with my kids. I can give away more money. I can stop over to visit that family in my neighborhood even if they might think I'm weird. I can risk getting turned down on my Ph.D. applications. I can face scary motorcycle rides, kids' sicknesses and even my own mortality. I don't have to cling to my life now because I know there is another.

After a woman we knew died in South Africa, we had a number of conversations with our kids about death and heaven. We had just visited the United States and driven from Wisconsin to Georgia to visit friends at Jubilee Partners. "Is heaven as far as Georgia?" Zeke asked one night. The question took me by surprise, and I spent a long time savoring it afterward. I liked thinking that going to heaven is like a little road trip to Georgia. It's a real, tangible place, not so very far away, and even more beautiful than the sun coming up over the woods in Georgia.

■　　■　　■

In countries where people don't have all the safety regulations and lawyers we have here in the United States, it's not that they don't dislike death as much as we do. The difference is that death is not unknown. When we fear death, we fear death plus fearing the unknown. We don't tell our children about death. We hide it. We cry quietly at funerals. We do not learn of a neighbor's death by hearing a woman run down the street wailing.

When Isaiah asks what to tell people, God says to tell them, "All people are like grass. . . . The grass withers and the flowers fall" (Isaiah 40:6-7). That's not what we want to hear from God. Yes, our days here are numbered. And that sucks, especially if we get to the end and don't like how we used those days.

Life is a complicated word in the Bible. It means, like we pretty much all can understand, the usual physical life that keeps the hospital heart monitor blipping. It also means the eternal life, the kind of life that comes by faith, the living forever in that place called heaven, near God, knowing God, with no more tears, forever and ever and ever. That kind of life we generally think is something we flip over into on the day the cancer or car accident shuts down our lungs and heart. It's the "next life."

There's more to the word *life*, though. At the start of the Bible when Adam and Eve disobeyed God and decided they should eat the forbidden fruit instead of trusting God, the consequence God promised for their disobedience was this: "When you eat from it you will certainly die" (Genesis 2:17). They didn't die in the sense of stopping breathing. Not at all. So did God lie about them surely dying? There's got to be another sort of death, a spiritual death that we can walk around in right now even if our lungs are pumping air. That kind of death includes hopelessly walking around believing life is just a few dumb decades and then you're gone forever. It means living far from God, unable to even fathom the joy and fulfillment you're missing. It means wasting this ordinary adventure called life.

Usually Jesus and God and angels in the Bible are telling people not to fear. Once, though, Jesus told people what they *should* fear. "Do not be afraid of those who kill the body and after that can do no more," Jesus told his friends. "But I will show you whom you should fear: Fear him who, after your body has been killed, has authority to throw you into hell. Yes, I tell you, fear him" (Luke 12:5).

The one thing, or person rather, we *are* supposed to fear, is God. That's who's in charge of our ultimate destiny. God won't put up with us living worthless lives full of empty stuff, and we should fear that kind of empty life so badly that we clutch our hands and legs and toes on tight to any safety net keeping us from it, as if we're suspended from the Golden Gate Bridge. Fortunately we do have a safety net to cling to, a really big strong one God made. It's called the gospel, the good news, the best news, and it isn't complicated. You admit you need Jesus, that you're a wreck (like everybody else). You acknowledge that God is your Creator, your divine Dad, and that Jesus died and then was alive again so that we can start enjoying the appetizers of real life *now* and the full-on banquet when our flesh rots. That's the good news that beats the eternal death, of which physical death is a symbol and a symptom. It's not complicated.

What is complicated is living out that gospel. Once we're alive we have to live alive. We have to get off our butts and put on our shoes. We have to notice God here, in the in-between, in the medium of life that is today.

■   ■   ■

My great aunt died at the age of ninety-four. My mom said, "She lived a full life." Most of us would consider ninety-four years a pretty full life, but it got me thinking, does just living that many years guarantee a life is full?

The same night, I read an email from a dear South African friend who has adopted several children and who works as a lawyer in Johannesburg. She wrote about how she views her life:

So here I am, at thirty-seven years of age, with the honour and privilege of having lived life richly and life having revealed and unfolded itself to me in ways that make me truly grateful. A

Catholic monk called Richard Rohr says that for many people, embracing death is a process that they are unwilling to contemplate and that, contrary to fundamentalist Christian thought and belief, many people are not unwilling to die because they are scared of hell or whatever else is there in the hereafter. Rather, says Richard Rohr, the angst comes from the sense that whatever it is that life is supposed to have been about, more often times than not, people feel that they have not touched "it" yet. They feel that they have not fully lived yet, that they have not sucked the marrow, so to speak. When I read that, I realized I was, by the grace of God, fully living life, and that I was ready to die, if that was my fate, because I had touched "it." I will admit that this audacious "project" of living life, has come with much struggle and pain, many tears, sleepless nights and much wrestling with what this is all about. I have died a thousand deaths and just when I thought I could die no more, I have died again.

I read and reread my friend's email that night. Her line about sucking the marrow out of life reminded me of sitting in my dorm room years earlier reading my American Literature class homework and finding that same phrase in Henry David Thoreau's book *Walden:* "I went to the woods because I wished to live deliberately . . . and not, when I came to die, discover that I had not lived. . . . I wanted to live deep and suck out all the marrow of life."[12]

I wanted to live deep and suck out the marrow of life too, even at the age of nineteen. Now, at age thirty-three, was I still sucking out the marrow? Could I say along with my friend that I had, by the grace of God, touched "it"? Had I lived "a pretty full life" every day and every year, whether life lasted for me thirty-three, sixty-five or ninety-four years?

■   ■   ■

Over a year later, I would sit in the same hospital in a different room—the waiting room of the intensive care unit. I would wait not for my own prognosis, but for my mom's.

My dad had called that Friday afternoon, his voice badly shaking, telling me to pray as the doctors rushed my mom into brain surgery. A massive aneurysm had burst in her brain.

Eight years before, a similar thing had happened to my mom. That time the bleeding was less, but recovery had involved four months of dizziness, nausea and vomiting, headaches and hypersensitivity to sounds and smells. My dad and I had both heard her say she never wanted to live through that again. She would rather just go home to heaven.

And so, as my dad and I sat in the waiting room during her surgery—as it dragged on for two, four and finally eight long hours— we talked about how it feels not to know what to pray. The doctors had made it clear that the operation was risky, but without it she could not live. Most people did not survive this. The fact that my father had been with her when it happened, that they had been only five minutes from a hospital, that she recognized what was happening immediately—all these improved her chances and indeed looked like miracles in themselves. But no one could predict anything. She might die. Or she might live, but what kind of life? Who knew what might be swept away—speech, movement, coherency?

She had lived a full life. She had touched "it." So what was left now, especially if life meant constant daily suffering?

I knew it wasn't hers to decide, or mine, or the doctor's, or any person's. God was all in charge now.

The next day, she woke up. She could feel and move her legs, her arms. She could talk. Everything worked. Doctors and nurses kept dropping the word *miraculous.*

For the first week in the hospital, as the swelling slowly released and her brain recovered, she was still confused much of the time. She would wake up and demand to go home, pulling her IV lines out and forgetting that she was there for her own brain surgery. On the second day after her surgery she told my dad, "I want to go home. But I have decided to stay a little longer."

I assumed she was talking about their house, but it could just as well have described her life here on earth. She would be here for some time longer. She knew her Savior well and would be happy to move home with him, but for some reason only he knew, not yet. However arduous the recovery process, however surgery may have changed her life even permanently, God did not leave her here to punish her or to test or torment her.

Three days after the surgery, just before I left her room, she asked, "Now what were we doing? Were we going to pray?"

Well, we hadn't been, but I said, "Sure, let's pray."

She went first, charging into it, thanking God for *my* life. She said not a word about herself, probably completely forgetting she had nearly died. She finished, "And God, save many people."

This woman, with hundreds of people praying for *her*, woke up and prayed for everyone but herself.

Her life is not by accident.

None of our lives are.

■　　■　　■

In my own emergency room visit awaiting my heart tests, I sat in the hospital scribbling thoughts of life and death on the only sheet of paper I had with me, a guide to the citywide rummage sales that weekend. I ran out of paper around nine at night, so I gave in and picked up the television remote. What is a person supposed to watch when they're waiting to hear if they're dying? I flipped through some cartoons, a *Rescue 911* episode and a crime drama. Then I saw the opening of *America's Funniest Home Videos* and stopped.

The announcer promised cheerfully, "Guaranteed to make you smile!" I knew people say laughter is the best medicine, so I decided to put them to the test. I watched a cat singing "Twinkle, Twinkle, Little Star." Then came a whole series of people falling off chairs and a series of people getting cakes in their faces. I watched a mom tumble down a children's bouncy slide and squash a kid. I forgot the little bleeps on the monitor to my right and the test results in a lab somewhere down the hall.

The Bible says, "Perfect love drives out fear" (1 John 4:18). God is that perfect love, and it's his forgiving grace that obliterates our ultimate fear of meaninglessness. In a day-to-day way, though, laughter also helps. I suppose laughter is one of the many weapons in God's armory against fear.

Then the doctor came in. All my test results had come out fine. My ribs were just tired from weeks of coughing and fighting off a cold. "Don't feel stupid," he told me. "It's good you came in. You can go home now and sleep well."

Just before I left, the nurse came to check my vital signs one last time. I got to watch the flat line on the heart monitor turn into a little blip of a triangle that moved across the screen. More triangles formed and moved. I said to the nurse, "It's good to know you're alive."

On my way out of the hospital, I passed some parents whose baby had a gash across her forehead. They were comforting her in Spanish. I saw a girl in a wheelchair staring blankly at a television, still wearing a sports uniform. Three people holding hands were talking in quiet voices, as if recounting how some accident happened, how some friend ended up behind the emergency room doors, how life went so suddenly from what it always was to something different. I thought of all the people who wouldn't walk out emergency room doors tonight, how it could have been otherwise for me.

Then I walked out the sliding doors.

My triangle blips are still moving, but every day might be the last day of my short mission trip here on earth. This is the only chance I get to pay attention, say what needs saying, do what needs doing. This is life, right here while the mail piles up and the kids need wiping and the dishwasher breaks. *This* is the day I was spared for, the amazing day, the amazing moment. Here with wet laundry in my hand and a husband coming home from work and kids spreading paper scraps across the floor and the garden dying because the nozzle of the hose broke—this is where I live that full life free of fear. The medium we paint with is today, and we don't get any other option.

ORDINARY ADVENTURES
in Overcoming Fears

- Do a cartwheel.
- People-watch in a hospital lobby.
- Choose a song you want sung at your funeral.
- Ride a merry-go-round.
- Laugh to tears.
- Write a letter to yourself and seal it to open in ten years.
- Climb a tree.
- Write a list of your biggest fears and burn it.
- Donate blood.
- Tell your closest friend how much you appreciate them.

DRAGONFLY
RESURRECTIONS

CHOOSING
Adam

At a rural home we lived in for two years in South Africa, I often went for walks early in the morning. Our landlord cultivated pecans, and tall grasses grew in the fields surrounding the rows upon rows of trees. In the winter, the mountain mornings were chilly with frost coating the grasses. In the summer, dew would drip off the grasses as the breezes started in the slanting sunshine.

One morning, I noticed drops of dew seemingly floating above a brilliant pink flower. As I walked closer, I realized the drops were suspended on the wings of a motionless dragonfly, poised on the beautiful flower.

In the sunrise, the dew sparkled on membrane wings, the dragonfly's yellow body with green

Morning walks can hold amazing details like this dew-covered dragonfly.

eyes resting on a brilliant pink blossom, against the lush green floor and the azure sky. I realized the dragonfly was dead. This little corpse was one of the most beautiful things I'd ever seen. I examined it from every side, walking around it, careful not to disturb the flower's stem. I pulled my camera off my shoulder and snapped a frame of it, trying to do justice to the exquisite, delicate surprise.

I started back home, still shaking my head in awe at the dazzling little creature. Halfway home I decided I should really take more pictures of it—to capture it, to share it. So I turned around and walked back.

It was gone.

There were no predators around, no one else walking on the desolate farm, no birds in the sky, no rodents scuttling about. I was alone with the pink flower.

A dragonfly resurrection.

I strolled home, thinking about the ephemeral beauty I had the privilege to glimpse. It was a small thing, sure, but I was not going to take it for granted. Just as this little creature that seemed dead in the weeds rose and flew away, my ordinary day had come alive and taken wings.

I walked home pondering what it takes for these kinds of resurrections to happen. Too often my brain is focused on the jagged anxiety *du jour* or on some shallower part of life. If I extricate myself from normal ruts, I often find things to observe or experiences that are intriguing, that are extraordinary. Sometimes, these little resurrections are just a matter of being attentive and noticing. Other times, I have to respond.

■   ■   ■

When we lived in South Africa, Chrissy gave me a weekend away on our motorcycle, alone, for my birthday. I planned and read and talked to people and researched routes with varied landscapes, roads and cultures. As I dreamed, an idea dawned on me for a great trip.

The idea came with a great title: "8 in 8: Eight Countries in Eight Days." Once I convinced Chrissy (not an easy sell, considering she'd have to take off work to watch the kids alone for over a week), selling articles about it to magazine editors was easy.

I rode from our home in KwaZulu-Natal, South Africa, up across Swaziland, north through half of Mozambique, across Zimbabwe, west through half of Zambia, along the Caprivi Strip in Namibia, before turning south across Botswana and Lesotho on my way back home.

At the time, Zimbabwe was in a tailspin. On the morning I would reach Zimbabwe, I started riding at 5:00 a.m., hoping to reach the border station before the line grew huge. Already when I got there, miles of semis were camped out along the highway leading in to the immigration office building and surrounding parking lot. Smaller vehicles parked and lined up inside the chainlink fence. I took about two hours to fill out multiple forms, wait in multiple lines, talk my way past two officials, and pay a bribe of three dollars

Always ready with a camera, Adam lies on the ground to shoot a lizard scurrying under our truck in a game park.

and some cigarettes. Then I was flying down the road again.

I stopped for a lunch meeting with a banker in the capital who was trying to find a way to support his family because he couldn't feed them on his bank salary. He was paid in Zimbabwean dollars, which were hyper inflated, at a rate of 215,000 percent for the year, so by the end of any month when he was supposed to receive his few hundred dollars' worth of pay, he would be lucky if the pay was

THIS ORDINARY ADVENTURE

enough to buy a cabbage.[13] Later, I pulled in at a gas station with my
fuel tank almost empty and learned that the station (like all the sta-
tions) was out of gas. The lonely attendant directed me to a house in
a back alley where I bought fuel from a barrel, paying in U.S. dollars.

So as I sped along the highway on the afternoon of my second day
on the road, I was a bit stressed.

I was praying as I baked inside my helmet and crash jacket,
sweating through my T-shirt. I asked God to get me through Zimbabwe, for my gas to last, that I'd avoid significant shakedowns at
police checkpoints, that the banker I met with would be able to feed
his family. Heat radiated off the blacktop, and I imagined my tires
steadily shedding tread in the rubber-melting temperatures, so I
prayed about that too.

Out in the distance, from the scrub brush and jacaranda trees, I
saw a headlight—a single headlight—indicating another member of
the motorcycle fraternity. As I hurtled toward my counterpart, I
could tell he wasn't going very fast, perhaps forty-five miles per hour
on the open highway. His machine was a Suzuki TS185, a minimalist
machine compared to my Honda TransAlp 650. His bike's engine
wasn't much to start with, and it was probably worn down by years
of hard work. It may have been the same model that Chrissy rode on
in Kenya behind Mike while rushing to make her bus.

It's customary for motorcyclists to give a little salute of some sort
when we pass one another—the left arm drops down and points to
the centerline (or gives a little wave if you're on the left side of the
road in a former British colony), or the helmet dips a bit toward the
other rider.

But on this two-lane desolate road in the middle of Zimbabwe,
my two-wheeled brother didn't nod his 1970s-style helmet or give a
little wave with his hand.

He let go.

On a bumpy highway, on a little clapped-out old motorcycle, with
only a T-shirt and providence keeping him from leaving a streak of

skin across the rough roadway, he let go of the handlebars and lifted his arms up wide. It could have been a moment of hilarity and goofiness from a young man just enjoying his ride, but it felt like a welcoming embrace for the lonely foreigner.

I had to reply. I never let a wave go past me without acknowledgment—it's the creed of two wheels. A wave wouldn't reply to this bold, risky greeting. A nod wasn't commensurate with his passion and risk. My mind raced, calculating my speed, the road surface and upcoming curves, and remembering what I learned about centrifugal force in my high school physics course with Mr. Brielmaier. In a split second we would be past one another, me pushing on toward Zambia and he puttering away to his life in the wringer of Zimbabwe.

I let go.

I dropped the throttle, sat up tall, threw my arms out wide and whooped into my helmet. And two men from different continents whooshed past each other, in a duet of risk for a moment of pure shared joy.

It was a small thing, a tiny moment among a million. I could have been calculating how many hours until I slept again, if I had enough fuel to get through Zimbabwe, when I'd have cell reception to try to call Chrissy and the kids, or any one of a number of other very important things.

Rather I had my eyes up. And when I saw something amazing, even just a small thing, I got to respond and join in, letting go of all the very important things. And rather than just praying to get through Zimbabwe, I was noticing how God was there.

■   ■   ■

I've gone through some similarly desperate prayers lately. The lease on our little apartment was running out at the end of April. So we made one last attempt to get an offer accepted on the house we loved so much up on the hill, with the woods and fields around it. It really, really felt like this was the place for us. Just in case, we added a contingency to the offer that we could move in before closing and rent the place until the deal was finalized. The sellers seemed unwilling to budge on anything else. So a month before we had to leave the apartment, the sellers agreed. We didn't close in time, but we moved in and started renting on Good Friday.

Reality sunk in that we then had to start figuring out what to do with this land. Two-and-a-half acres feels like a lot of dirt. This was the first time we had to wrestle with how to steward a patch of earth properly, and we believed doing so mattered much to God and our souls.

Just after we started renting, we invited over an older couple from our neighborhood to help us dream up ways to best care for our land for generations to come. The husband is a renowned expert in environmental ethics and land stewardship from the university. He stood next to our lone bur oak tree and patted its bark, looking up into its branches with admiration. These bur oaks, he explained, are the foundation of oak savanna, an ecosystem that once covered as much as 75 percent of the landscape in southern Wisconsin where we live. The oak savanna ecosystems have become one of the most threatened plant communities in the Midwest, and many of the plants that grow only in the dappled sunlight of oak savannas are also endangered. Our newly rented home sits next to state land where oak savanna restorations are already underway.

"You can plant another oak tree over here," our friend said, pointing to an open space where we planned to take out an invasive tree. "It'll grow up in no time."

His wife caught my eye and gave a quizzical smile at his words. She whispered, "In no time? Maybe in, oh, about twenty years."

Maybe for him, a professor old enough to retire, who had spent his life involved in local politics, protecting thousands of acres of natural landscape, who had trained thousands of students in creation care, who had worked with his wife to shape their own property into a beautiful respite for birds, wildlife and soul-weary visitors, who had seen what's possible in a lifetime of steady choices made well, maybe for him this oak tree will mature "in no time." From this side it doesn't feel that easy.

If we want oak trees, we need to plant acorns, one by one.

We have one *quercus macrocarpa* on our new land, that precious bur oak. It's about twenty-five years old, but its trunk is only a few inches thick. Bur oaks grow up to one hundred twenty feet. They live up to four hundred years. And their trunks can grow to be ten feet across.

By God's providence or the thoughtfulness of a forerunner on this parcel, we have that one bur oak tree. Let's say our children gather up some acorns and plant them in our dirt. In a year they'll be tall enough to wrap with a plastic tube so the deer don't eat them off. If we live here twenty-five years, they'll be nice smallish trees. Even if we live here the rest of our lives, they won't be close to fully grown.

But we plant them anyway.

■   ■   ■

Today, I can notice the little amazing things around me and I can respond. I can take steps and make plans that will grow almost imperceptibly. I can make some small decisions that will have big effects, like sticking tiny acorns in the earth. When I'm gray and wrinkly, if God grants me that grace, I'll enjoy watching the sun rise behind oaks rather than across an open field. I'll look back on my life and see how small decisions and tiny steps began some very big adventures. I hope to see the results of a life well-lived: my gray, wrinkly and smiling bride; two kids living well in the world; a church filled with people I've known for decades and people who've just come in; projects and ministries that we supported with our money and time; and friends who I got to see start on this ordinary adventure with Jesus. It's doubtful I'll see all of these slow-growing fruits from seeds planted now, but surely I'll see some of them.

This is a terribly big deal, and it makes me tremble again. Am I really willing to consider everything—my dreams, my plans, my education, my job, my free time, my money, my friendships, my marriage, my parenting, my house—in light of God's amazing calling on my life that should still be affecting the world ten, twenty-five, even a hundred years from now? Will I do what is necessary to prepare the ground for a field of oaks that will drop their own acorns, seeding and reseeding in generations of resurrections? Do I have the foresight and the patience—the faith—to find the best acorns and stick them in the dirt?

■   ■   ■

When I despair at the long, slow ordinary adventure, I stop and remember. While I'm not an old man yet, I've already been planting acorns long enough to see a few oak saplings stretching toward the sun. We asked people to not give us gifts for our wedding, so we could live simply and travel light. We drove rusty little cars and got our furniture from curbs and coffee shops, so we could easily ditch them when Jesus took us overseas. We lived in tiny (and sometimes rat-infested) homes, bonding with our neighbors. A series of boring phone calls and meetings landed a coffee deal for Raúl and our other friends there. We got our master's degrees in international development so we would have the knowledge and credibility to do more good for people in hard places. We learned from simple people around the world as Phoebe slept on tables, floors, trains and planes and Zeke happily somersaulted around the world with only a handful of toys. We tried the family sports group and started a handful of good friendships. God has graciously built into us habits of noticing small amazing things every day, responding wholeheartedly and taking small steps for long-term effect, and that makes a difference. No one said this was going to be easy. When people hear a part of our story and say, "That's amazing! I would *so* love to do that!" they're not usually talking about loneliness, malaria, failure, motorcycle accidents, anxiety, pick-pocketing, crosscultural stress, fleas, self-doubt and lice.

■   ■   ■

Napoleon was right when he said, "Nothing is more difficult and therefore the more precious than the ability to decide." Living this ordinary adventure requires some moments (or days or years) of risk, discomfort, frustration and the rest, but sometimes worse than any actual hardship is the agony of making all the decisions life puts in our path.

In order to notice dragonflies, or throw my arms out with "reckless abandon" (to quote Oswald Chambers), or plant acorns, I need to make some decisions. I have to take in life's options and decide what the right response to what I'm seeing is. What are the right acorns to plant today to grow the right kind of tree?

Sometimes I complicate decisions. Jesus is more extreme than any human I've heard of, both in courage and compassion, in love and in truth, in acceptance and judgment. Knowing Jesus is the easiest thing in the world, and following him is the hardest. I need to give God my desire to decrease in selfishness, trying my best but relying on grace. For me, it's essential that I spend time studying and imagining myself into the lives scribbled across the Bible, and spend some time with this wild fellow Jesus. When I do that, I usually find clarity in what acorns to plant today or which fork to take in the road. It's when I try to hang on to my own petty visions that I get confused.

When we face decisions in life that feel big, like what house or country to live in or what job to apply for, Chrissy and I sometimes recall a conversation from a dozen years earlier. We were thinking about getting engaged, and Chrissy met to talk with a woman named Renae who worked with the campus ministry. Her words have stuck with us as wisdom for many situations since: "If you make all the little choices faithfully, the big choices don't feel so big." Sure enough, after many long conversations about trying to honor God with our relationship as we dated, the marriage step felt like just another footprint on the path we'd already been walking. By paying attention to God as we make all the million little decisions of life, we can slowly rudder a course that takes us closer to our Creator and King, toward the life that celebrates him.

When we started renting the house, there was just one bur oak. Our friend soon had us scheming about where to plant more acorns. We were also choosing the right baby steps for many kinds of oaks that we hoped to see grow in this home: choosing the place, negotiating the final house purchase details and simply waiting. Those were the acorns we put in the ground here, and we prayed they would sprout and grow for many years.

I trust that if I'm doing well on the acorn end, I'll end up with some big ol' oaks.

ORDINARY ADVENTURES
in Choosing

- Take a walk every day for a month.
- Put your feet in a lake, river or ocean.
- Brush your teeth outside.
- Take a bath every day for a month.
- Meet weekly with a group of friends to talk about the important stuff.
- Job shadow someone with the job you might want.
- Take a photograph every day for a month.
- Write a personal mission statement.
- Take a retreat.
- Plant a tree.

Epilogue

LA CELEBRACIÓN
Adam and Chrissy

One afternoon in Nicaragua we sat in our friend Juana's house keeping her company as she finished tortillas for dinner. She flipped a tortilla over on the metal tractor cultivator disc that served as a griddle over her fire, then reached down to slap the side of a huge pig that often nosed its way into her open-sided kitchen.

"When are we going to eat that pig?" Chrissy asked jokingly.

"No, no. This one we're not eating yet. This pig has a story." She proceeded to tell us a story far better than our entertaining attempts at the "The Three Billy Goats Gruff." "This pig," she tossed him a ball of tortilla dough, "is for our *celebración*."

Two years earlier, in October 1998, Hurricane Mitch had swept across the country of Nicaragua. At the time it was the strongest Atlantic October hurricane ever recorded. Places in Central America recorded up to seventy-five inches of rainfall. Around eleven thousand people died. Among them were over two thousand people who were buried when a ten-mile-wide patch of mountainside collapsed just one mountain north along the range where we would live in El Porvenir.

As the hurricane hit, our friends in El Porvenir were fighting for their lives. Pounding rains fell constantly for over a week. Roadways filled with torrents of water that cut chasms fifteen feet deep into the hillside.

Our friend Juana's husband, Tomás, was on the way home from a visit to another village when the hurricane rains came. On his way he found himself trapped between flooding currents of water. Water surrounded him from all sides, and he saw death closing in.

Neighbors down the mountain heard Tomás screaming for help. They sent word to Juana. As she remembers their message, it was, "Tomás is going to die."

She knelt on the muddy floor of her home and prayed as she had never prayed before. She prayed. She waited. In time she assumed that her husband must already be gone.

Instead he walked into their home. He was drenched and exhausted, but 100 percent alive. Neighbors had found a rope to toss across the water and dragged him to safety through the torrent.

"For this," she looked at us solemnly, "we are thanking God."

Three months later, she and friends and family slaughtered that hog. They invited all the people in a couple of villages, hired musicians, rented a generator and amplifier, brought in a pastor from a neighboring village to preach, bought Coca-Cola and ice from town, and made buckets upon buckets of rice, beans, cabbage salad, beet salad and fried pork. Everyone ate. No one paid. The God who grants life was extravagantly, amazingly and deservedly celebrated.

That we would call a party of biblical proportions.

■ ■ ■

Not long after we moved into our rented house, still waiting for a closing, Adam was studying some passages by Luke in the Bible. He noticed a common theme, not often dwelt on: Jesus went to a lot of feasts and celebrations. Banquets pop up all over. Banquets by tax collectors, banquets for the rich and for the poor, banquets put on by God.

He read about those celebrations and thought, we're about due for a *celebración*, a party of biblical proportions. When we arrived in the United States we had no jobs, home, furniture, school, community, church or idea what our life in this country would look like. Now we had nearly all of those. About a year after Adam started his job with InterVarsity, Chrissy had heard news that she was accepted into the Cultural Anthropology Ph.D. Program at UW–Madison. She would spend the next five or more years studying and researching how to better understand and serve neighbors in diverse cultures around the world. Her research would bring us back to South Africa for short and long trips. Only one piece remained unplaced: the house.

All summer we waited. When the zoning changes were finally approved, the sellers' lender stalled on approval of the sale. Banks and real estate agents called with projected closing dates, and one after another, those dates slid past. Knowing we could still fail to close a deal on this house and have to leave at any time, we waited on long-term investments including a dishwasher, water softener, wood-burning stove and fruit trees. One afternoon Adam stood out in the driveway talking to the new neighbors who were trying to sell us the house, hearing how equally frustrated they were over the delayed deal. Adam offered to pray, and in a surreal moment they stood in the driveway together, distraught and asking God for help amidst their tears.

After a full eight-and-a-half months since we made our first offer on the house, we closed. We bought the house. We settled down, officially. (We had the debt to prove it.)

With all we'd seen God do in the past years, we were ready to pull out all the stops and crank up a *celebración* like Juana's.

We found a square dance caller to open the afternoon with dancing. We chainsawed logs to build benches around a new fire pit for s'mores to finish the evening. We invited everyone we could think of and asked everyone to bring the best food they could cook and the recipe to share. Adam went shopping and filled a large shopping cart with chicken and then returned for another cartload of wine and beer. Chrissy's brother Dan drove five hours to spend the weekend and help dust, vacuum, sweep, mop, unclutter and cook the mountain of chicken. Our friend Chris the baker stopped by with a surprise gift of several hundred spicy cheese bread rolls, a throwback to our own days playing Bread Fairy with huge sacks full of day-old artisan bread.

After church on the Sunday of the party, Dan stood at the end of the driveway ready to direct parking. The first guests strolled up the driveway and Adam launched a football into the air, aiming it at his co-

The Celebration of Biblical Proportions

worker, Gary, whom he had gotten to know sharing Jell-O stories more than a year before. Soon a game of soccer started in the front yard. A friend there with her granddaughter watched from the sidelines. "I've not played soccer in forty years, Adam!"

"But you have to, Linda—it's an Amazing Day!" Adam grabbed her hand and she joined the game.

Guests covered the yard, the porch, the living room, and food covered the three tables beside the house.

The square dance caller set up his little record player in a shelter in the nearby park, and two squares of eight people tentatively volunteered to try. Adam grabbed more from the sidelines and dragged them into another square. Our longtime friend Sue, who runs ropes courses and takes young people on outdoor adventures, sat with her boyfriend on a picnic table. "Challenge by choice," she shook her head, refusing to budge.

Dancers followed the caller, stomping in circles, holding hands, in and out and back around. The patterns grew more complicated and confidence grew. Children giggled as they learned to "do-si-do" and everyone joined in coaching them and swinging them in circles. Sue and her boyfriend stood up from the picnic table and smiled as they joined a circle, taking challenge by choice after all. When Adam and his partner took their turn in the center, he literally jumped for joy.

The square dance ended, and the chicken lay packed into a grill for a final roasting. Someone got a text warning that hail was on the way. A deep gray mass loomed over half the sky. We had no space in the house for the hundred-some guests who now roamed across the lawn. Rain or no rain, hail or no hail, this party must go on. If we could play Ultimate Frisbee with three-year-olds in the rain, surely we could feed a hundred people in rain.

Hungry children hovered with their faces inches above the three long tables, now packed with casseroles, breads, stews, cookies, Jell-O

Enormous bags of Twiggles (a South African version of Cheetos) were our contribution to many celebrations.

made especially by a coworker for Adam, pumpkin pie, recipes with stories and decades of history.

"Hey everybody, c'mon over!" Adam escaped the grill long enough to shout everyone together. "Before we eat, we need to say something."

We stepped up onto the top step leading onto the front porch.

In a few quick minutes while the children tried to keep their fingers out of the pistachios and cookies on the food tables, Adam recapped our time since returning from the United States. We arrived with so many question marks, and now we marveled at all God had provided: old and new friends, Adam's job, Chrissy's Ph.D. program, the children's new school, the house, the land, the place to stay at after all the moving. We told the story of Juana and her slaughtered pig, explained that barbecued chicken would have to do for us this time instead of a pig, but that the reasoning was the same. God had given us life, and we wanted to celebrate, like Juana and like Jesus.

"We're kinda ordinary now," Adam finished, "but we're going to keep having adventures. We thank God for our time overseas, for bringing us back here, for providing so well for us, and for great friends like you guys. Let's pray together and then eat this food!" And he prayed, giving thanks for the big day and the potluck spread.

An hour later we crossed paths in the midst of the mayhem. Silently we stood and looked around. The hail had passed us by without so much as a drip of rain. Everywhere, people were talking, laughing, holding drinks and plates. Pastors and

Sign in front of a South African home: "Praise God, Amen"

atheists, people of different ethnicities, ages and backgrounds chatted in bunches on lawn chairs, tarps and blankets on the grass, on couches and chairs inside, at stools in the kitchen, and standing everywhere. Beneath one giant old tree, four children shared our tire swing, one hanging on the rope, one on top of the tire and one at the bottom, with another pushing and everyone squealing in delight. Two sisters in fancy princess party dresses rolled on the ground. "We wear clothes to get them dirty," their mom smiled and shrugged. A group of neighbors from our street stood talking by the food table. A friend was tuning his guitar to sing through the evening. Someone had collected a dozen sticks from the forest and handed them out to children to roast marshmallows on the fire. Phoebe was teaching a friend how to walk on stilts, and Zeke was cracking open pistachio nuts in the food line.

"This was an Amazing Day." Adam let out a long sigh as we squeezed each other's hands.

And it was an Amazing Day. One of our most amazing to be sure. It would make a nice story to remember and tell, perhaps even a "wow story." But that was not the point.

The point was what—or rather who—we were celebrating. The same God we celebrated that day is alive among us and deserving of being celebrated every day. We are not on earth to impress somebody human; we are here to celebrate Somebody divine. And we can celebrate that Somebody as we drive to work, as we chat in a neighbor's kitchen, as we hold a two-year-old's hand across the grocery store parking lot, as we answer the forty-third email of the day, as we give a bike to someone living on the streets, as we pick tomatoes, clean toilets, take walks and share cashews. God is among us, never settling. He deserves far more from us than a passing glance as we sink into a couch.

As Eugene Peterson wrote:

Our stories may be interesting, but they are not the point. Our achievements may be marvelous, but they are not germane. . . . Bless God. Do that for which you were you were created and redeemed; lift your voices in gratitude; enter into the community of praise and prayer that anticipates the final consummation of faith in heaven. Bless God.[14]

Living like *that* is Amazing.

Discussion Questions

ONE: Dented Dishwashers *Becoming Ordinary*

1. In what ways do you think God is challenging you to get out of ruts you've been stuck in or to reshape your life? What holds you back?

2. Could you write something on your Amazing Days list today? What are you planning for tomorrow?

TWO: The Last Hurrah *Leaving Adventures Behind*

1. What have been high points in your life when you felt like you had "an espresso shot for the soul"? How did you keep your excitement from fading, or what might have kept it from fading?

2. The author asks how to be "faithful to the brooms, the vacuum cleaners, the paint brushes, web pages, libraries, picket fences, iPads, coffee cups, grocery carts, living rooms and whatever else we've been handed in life." What tools and skills have you been handed in life that you want to use well?

THREE: Faith Muscles *Getting Moving*

1. The author describes "trying to pray willy-nilly about stuff I only half cared about to some wishy-washy God who only half cared," and the hesitation that "never quite dares to ask for anything." How do your prayers compare to that?

2. What does it mean for you to have a faith that "puts on shoes"?

FOUR: Thorns and Thistles *Work*

1. What's your favorite memory of an elegant Jell-O dessert?

2. How have you experienced thorns and thistles in your current job? Which ones can you cut down? Which ones do you have to endure (and how can you)?

3. Imagine yourself imprisoned in a country where people are not allowed to confess faith in Jesus. Would you most likely be (a) scratching profanity and complaints into the cell walls, (b) looking for an easy way to denounce your faith, or (c) risking torture for the sake of your commitment to Jesus? How does this scenario compare to current challenges at your workplace?

FIVE: The Cool Table *Identity*

1. Were you cool in middle school?

2. When else have you experienced a hierarchy of cool or some other measure of your self-worth? What qualities or accomplishments do you feel the most pressure to conform to or pursue? Who do you feel evaluating you?

3. When have you seen examples in your own life or in someone else's life of living in the freedom of grace? In what aspects of your life do you need to rediscover that grace?

SIX: All I Got for Christmas Was Malaria *Suffering*

1. What does it mean to follow a God who suffered? How is that challenging? Comforting? (See Philippians 2:3-11.)

2. What trials are you facing that you need "to consider pure joy"?

SEVEN: Washing Machine Guilt *Money*

1. Are you more likely to tend toward legalistic frugality or wasteful

spending in your use of money? Are there changes you would like to make in how you use and regard money?

2. What examples can you think of from the Bible showing God's extravagance and generosity? What examples can you think of showing God's humility and poverty?

3. How can you cultivate contentment today?

EIGHT: The Honeymoon Never Ends *Marriage*

1. What examples have you seen of good or bad marriages? How do these shape what you want or don't want in marriage?

2. In what ways can a marriage compel people toward serving God? In what ways can marriage get in the way of serving God (for both single and married people)?

NINE: Baby Slaves *Parenting*

1. Do you know someone who might feel trapped by parenting, as if a Mommy or Daddy has tied up the person they want to be? How can you support them?

2. Have you seen fears about children's safety make people shirk hard calls from Jesus? Whether you have children now or might in the future, what are some commitments you want to make about how you (would) want to live as a parent?

3. Who is "in your circle" that you need to love well this week?

TEN: The Revolution *Community*

1. What are the biggest challenges you face in developing strong community?

2. Do you have the friendship you need? Is there something you would change about your friendships—for example, more deep

friendships and fewer shallow ones, more diverse ages or ethnic groups, more good role models, more people for whom you might become a role model, etc.?

ELEVEN: Putting on Underwear *Fear*

1. Tell the story of a time when you had to confront your mortality (or someone else's). How did that experience affect how you lived?

2. How have you witnessed the epidemic of fear in North America? How do you deal with that?

TWELVE: Dragonfly Resurrections *Choosing*

1. Describe a time when you noticed God's presence in some small or commonplace moment like a dragonfly resurrection.

2. What are some "very important things" that distract you from responding in the blink of an eye to amazing opportunities?

3. What examples do you see looking back at your life when God used your acorn-sized choices to make a significant difference? What steps do you anticipate taking in the next year that could have a similar lasting effect?

EPILOGUE: *La Celebración*

1. What was the best party you've ever attended? What made it great?

2. What suggestions have you tried, or do you plan to try, from the suggestions at the end of the chapters?

3. Does your life tend to be more "ordinary" or more "adventurous"? What steps do you want to take next in living out your ordinary adventure?

Notes

[1]Christine Jeske, *Into the Mud: Inspiration for Everyday Activists* (Chicago: Moody Press, 2010).

[2]Martin Luther King Jr, "Three Dimensions of a Complete Life," sermon given April 19, 1959, in Montgomery, Alabama. King's written notes are accessible at www.thekingcenter.org/archive/document/three-dimensions-complete-life#.

[3]Thomas Merton, *Thoughts in Solitude* (New York: Farrar, Straus & Giroux, 1956), p. 24.

[4]Ibid. Emphasis added.

[5]Ibid., pp. 51, 74.

[6]Anne Lamott, *Bird by Bird* (New York: Anchor, 1995), p. xxx.

[7]Merton, *Thoughts in Solitude*, p. 115.

[8]The sermon was by Tim Mackie at Blackhawk Church in Madison, Wisconsin.

[9]Willa Cather, *O Pioneers!* (Pleasantville, NY: Readers Digest, 1990).

[10]Dietrich Bonhoeffer, *Life Together: The Classic Exploration of Faith in Community* (New York: Harper and Row, 1954), p. 27.

[11]C. S. Lewis, *The Lion, the Witch, and the Wardrobe*, in *The Complete Chronicles of Narnia* (New York: HarperCollins, 1998), p. 99.

[12]Henry David Thoreau, *Walden and Civil Disobedience* (Rockville, MD: Manor, 2007), p. 56.

[13]Steve H. Hanke, "R.I.P. Zimbabwe Dollar," Cato Institute (2010), www.cato.org/zimbabwe.

[14]Eugene Peterson, *A Long Obedience in the Same Direction* (Downers Grove, IL: InterVarsity Press, 2000), pp. 193-94.

CONNECT AND SHARE

We are trying to continue living This Ordinary Adventure every day. Please connect with us and let us know about your Amazing Days! And if you've benefited from this book, please post about it and encourage your friends to read it—we could all use more allies on the journey, right?

ExecutingIdeas.com

IntoTheMud.com

 /Adam.Jeske

 /Christine.SorensenJeske

 /AdamJeske

 /ChristineJeske

We're excited to share more about our adventures, too. Let us know if you would like us to speak to your group.